uncles

uncles

A Tribute to
the Coolest Guys
in the World

RUSSELL WILD

CB
CONTEMPORARY BOOKS

Library of Congress Cataloging-in-Publication Data

Wild, Russell.
    Uncles : a tribute to the coolest guys in the world / Russell Wild.
       p.   cm.
    Includes bibliographical references.
    ISBN 0-8092-2663-4
    1. Uncles.   I. Title.
HQ759.94.W55 1999
306.87—dc21   99-14657
                                           CIP

Cover design by Monica Baziuk
Interior design by Scott Rattray

Published by Contemporary Books
A division of NTC/Contemporary Publishing Group, Inc.
4255 West Touhy Avenue, Lincolnwood (Chicago), Illinois
60712-1975 U.S.A.
International Standard Book Number: 0-8092-2663-4

99 00 01 02 03 04 LB 15 14 13 12 11 10 9 8 7 6 5 4 3 2 1

CONTENTS

INTRODUCTION: UNCLES, AUNTS, THIS BOOK, THAT BOOK

You have in your hands one part of a set. The other part, titled *Aunts,* was written by Annette Sara Cunningham. The cover of that book has a soft yellow background decorated with delicate little orange flowers. Open up the pages and you are ushered into the warm and cinnamony bosom of aunthood.

This book has no bosom. It has chest hair.

That's not to say that uncles can't be nurturing. Not at all. I've held my little nephews or niece close to comfort them. I've made them hot cocoa and blueberry pancakes and put Band-Aids on their little scraped knees. But, truth be told, most of the time I'm with my niece and nephews is spent casting them into the pool or hoisting them up in my arms, growling like a T-Rex and ripping pine needles off branches with huge T-Rex teeth. On more mellow occasions, the kids and I may be hunting fireflies, picking mulberries, flying a kite, or sharing scary stories.

Call me your everyday uncle.

And this book would probably be your everyday uncle book—if it weren't also, I do believe, the world's first uncle book! And what does the world's first uncle book have to offer? It is first and foremost a tribute to the uncle—Pugsley and Wednesday's, Buffy and Jody's, yours and mine. It is also a manual for how to be an uncle, with hints and suggestions on everything from gift giving and joke telling to boomerang throwing and recounting old war stories.

Finally, this book is the world's largest and finest repository of uncle trivia, from the story behind Uncle Sam and the legend of Uncle Ben (you don't want to know), to the disclosure of the location of the ultra-secret headquarters of that international crime-busting organization, U.N.C.L.E.

The only thing this book doesn't have is a bosom. Which is why it is part of a set.

Uncle Russ

Rwild@Compuserve.com

uncles

1

INITIATION INTO UNCLEHOOD

Uncles aren't born. Like cheese spread and lite beer, we're processed. The uncle process usually starts with the birth of a sister or brother who grows up, falls in love, marries, works at several dumb jobs, then decides something is missing in life, and so has a child—maybe two or three.

In the meantime, you've been doing pretty much the same thing with your life, which has kept you quite busy, so that for the past several years you likely haven't done much more than exchange crummy holiday cards with your sibling. Then one night you get a call (usually from your parents). "Congratulations!" say Mom and Dad. "You just became an uncle."

I have one sister, Nancy, who married a nice guy named Jon Littman, and they have two children, Jeffrey and Melissa. I call them "Jeffreyburger" and "Melissapissa." Don't ask why. I don't know. Jeffreyburger and Melissapissa are being raised in the tropical ultrahumidity of southern Florida. Not only am I uncle to the soggy but wonderful Littman kids, but Jon is "Uncle Jon" to my own two great children, Clay and Addie.

There are other processes whereby any mere mortal male can become an uncle. You can, for instance, marry a woman who has a sibling who decides to have a child, and then one night you get a call (usually from your wife's parents). My wife, Susan, has a sister, Danielle, and she married a decent fellow named Patrick McDonald, and they also have two children. The McDonald boys are Clancy ("Cwancy") and Liam ("Baby Liam"). Cwancy and Baby Liam live on the outskirts of Baltimore. Cwancy and Clay are very close in age (now six), which means that when they get together they are alternatively best friends and worst enemies, but mostly best friends.

Uncles aren't always brother or sister to Mom or Dad. In many families, like mine, cousins who skip generations may refer to their much older male cousins as uncles. If I refer later in this book to my Uncle Larry, Uncle Jerry, or Uncle Sid, they're really—technically and genealogically speaking—my first cousins once removed. But since they are my parents' age, drive four-door American cars, and wear brimmed hats, I've always thought of them, and always will think of them, more like uncles than cousins.

In similar fashion, I would hope that cousins more of my children's generation—Alecia, Alex, Amanda, Deborah, Emma, Gregory, Neil, Tyler, Jonah, Julia, Ryan, Susie, and others I have yet to meet—might consider me something of an uncle.

Uncles don't necessarily have to be blood relatives. My close friends whom I've known since high school (they were high school sweethearts) are Nancy and Bobby Ippolito. They have two boys, Gregory ("Greggums") and Stephen ("Stevarino"), who grew up calling me "Uncle Russ," still call me Uncle Russ, and I hope always will call me Uncle Russ. Greggums and Stevarino live in southern California, pretty far from Pennsylvania, but we still manage to get together about twice a year, and we talk often.

The last route to unclehood is more calculated than the rest. Many men have found a youngster on their own, perhaps through a "rent-a-kid" agency like Big Brother/Big Sister (BBBS), or in foster care, and the youngster then becomes a de facto nephew or niece. I was for many years a Big Brother to a boy named Herminio Caraballo, who is now a young man. I've always felt like an uncle around him.

You can do the same as I did, if you wish. I'd recommend you do it through Big Brother/Big Sister; I can't say enough good things about the organization. If you're interested in finding out more, you can look up BBBS in your local phone book; if you're computerized, check out www.bbbsa.org on the Web. To find other groups in your area that may help you "adopt" a niece or nephew, contact Kids Campaigns at 1-888-544-5437, or visit www.kidscampaigns.org in cyberland.

You can also offer to care for a friend's or neighbor's child from time to time. Or call a local public school or community organization and ask about coaching or tutoring a youngster in need.

UNCLE RELATIONSHIPS: WHAT'S IN IT FOR THE LITTLE ONES?

Boys and girls need men in their lives. Unfortunately, Dad's not always in the picture. And even when Dad is in the picture, he is often working long hours. If Mom works long hours, too, then the little ones most often wind up with Grandma or in day care. Many day-care centers, such as the one my children attend, have a loving, caring, intelligent staff, which happens to be nearly all women. Just try finding a man in a typical day-care classroom. They are as rare as pearls in clams. Even when the child starts elementary school, a good male role model is still awfully hard to find.

Enter the uncle.

I'm fairly certain that most uncles are wholly unaware of how much their nephews and nieces look up to them. When I was nine or so, my Uncle Irv (married to my father's sister) came in from the West Coast to stay with us in Long Island for a few days. I remember it as a glorious time. Uncle Irv walked the dog with me; kicked around balls in the backyard; and told my sister and me stories of the tar pits, Disneyland, sunsets over the ocean, and other attractions of the Magical Kingdom of California.

In my interviews with youngsters about their uncles, I was struck time and time again by the degree to which children revere their uncles. Says Brittany, fifteen, "My Uncle Craig is like one of my favorite guys in the world. He doesn't get all bent out of shape by every little thing. And he seems to know at least a little something about everything! When I need someone to talk to, Uncle Craig always listens, and he doesn't come back at me, like some adults, like my parents, with dumb advice."

Uncles have very special significance to children around the holiday season. Says Ryan, sixteen, "It was always my Uncle Mark or my Uncle Steve who got dressed up as Santa and came to our house on Christmas morning. Who could make a better Santa than an uncle?!"

The importance of uncles doesn't end when a child grows up and no longer believes in Santa. As men's movement leader Robert Bly points out whenever he breaks from drumming, young men need older men— the more the better—to show them the ropes and rope burns of life. Young men aren't the only ones who need a male mentor. As I learned in my interviews of many nieces (some of whose stories you'll read later), uncles can often be among the most supportive and influential men in the lives of young women, as well.

UNCLE RELATIONSHIPS: WHAT'S IN IT FOR THE BIG GUYS?

Ah, the pitter-patter of little feet, the flash of a child's smile, the ways that little ones help us to reconnect with the world around us. Then, when those little angels get tired and cranky and their pants begin showing signs of strange deposits within, you hand them back to their parents! Could anything on earth be as wonderful as a little niece or nephew?

Yes—an *older* niece or nephew. For as they grow, our nieces and nephews can become true friends, sharing with us the joys and sorrows of life, helping to provide us with a sense of family and belonging often truly appreciated only by those who lack it. I consider my growing niece and nephews to be real buddies, and I intend to keep it that way forever.

WHERE UNCLES APPEAR ON THE FAMILY TREE

Note that, despite common belief, it is not necessary to be a sports fanatic or to drink beer in order to be an uncle, although in practice that often seems to be the case.

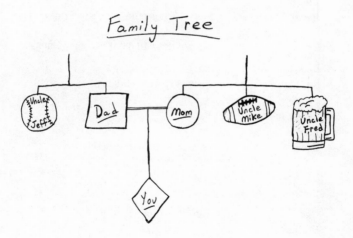

How to Tell an Uncle from the Other Important Men in Your Life

Let's face it, uncles are different than dads. They're looser. They're cooler. They're more regular guys. Come to think of it, uncles are different from all the other men we love. Here's a snapshot of those differences, or at least the most important ones.

1. Can you hit him up for money?

Dad	That's what dads are for!
Brother	Forget about it.
Buddy	Up to $5.
Father-in-law	On a very good day.
Clergy	Nah.
Uncle	Possibly, if you get him on a Friday.

2. Can you talk to him about politics without it getting personal?

Dad	Not usually.
Brother	*Everything* gets personal.
Buddy	Sometimes.
Father-in-law	Ha!
Clergy	Iffy.
Uncle	Does getting a wedgie qualify as "personal"?

3. Can you swap fart jokes with him?

Dad	Depends on socioeconomic background.
Brother	Yes, absolutely.

Buddy	Of course.
Father-in-law	No, no, no.
Clergy	Not a very good idea.
Uncle	Perfect!

4. Is he good for watching NBA play-offs with?

Dad	Yes.
Brother	Yes.
Buddy	If *he* brings the beer.
Father-in-law	Not bad.
Clergy	No (you don't want to have to watch your damned language).
Uncle	Ideal!

5. What's an appropriate item to give him for Christmas or Hanukkah?

Dad	Tie with little sailboats.
Brother	Timex watch.
Buddy	The $5 you borrowed back in May.
Father-in-law	Sweater (brown).
Clergy	Hallmark card.
Uncle	Whoopie cushion.

2

TRULY ESSENTIAL
UNCLE MISCELLANEA

There are no courses on uncles in America's schools and universities. Books on uncles (until this one appeared) haven't been available, even through rare book dealers. And neither PBS nor the Discovery Channel, to this author's knowledge, has ever done a single special on uncles. Is it any wonder then that most Americans are woefully ignorant on the subject of unclehood?

Consider this chapter your remedial education. We'll start with the important role that uncles play in our language and proceed from there to look at uncles in history, literature, government, poetry, and foreign relations.

ON SURRENDERING TO A
MONKEY'S UNCLE

The word "uncle" comes from the Latin *avunculus*, which in Roman days referred specifically to one's mother's brother, who typically wore a soiled toga, drove an old-model chariot, and had season passes to the Colosseum games. From Latin, the word moved into Old French, where it fermented for several centuries before slipping very cunningly into medieval English. Given the lack of decent spell-check programs in pre-Microsoft England, the word took on various whacked-out forms such as *unckle, unkel, vnkel, unkell, unkil, hunckyl, oncyll, ownkyll, onkill, uncull,* and *unckall.*

The first use of the modern spelling, according to the venerable *Oxford English Dictionary,* came in 1387, when someone named Trevisa wrote "Alisaundre exiled dwelled awhile wiþ his uncle in Epirus." Trevisa's descendants are still trying to collect royalties on that sentence, and Alisaundre's uncle was last seen sipping margaritas in the lobby of the Acropolis Hilton. In the meanwhile, the word "uncle" has been standardized, deodorized, and ushered into the modern dictionary, wedged rather unceremoniously between "unclassified" and "unclean."

"Uncle" has also wriggled its way into several eminent English expressions, such as "say uncle," "monkey's uncle," "Dutch uncle," "Uncle Tom," and "Bob's your uncle."

• "*Say* (or *cry*) *uncle*" means to surrender or admit defeat. My friend Sue Nowacki, of St. Augustine, Florida, tells of how the expression is used in her family:

I only had one uncle, Uncle Bud. When my brothers would tickle me, get me in a wrestle hold, or otherwise harass me, I would yell, "Uncle!" to which they'd always inquire, "Uncle who?" and I'd have to respond, "Uncle Bud!" I remember saying that name with very little air to breathe. Now, when I tickle, wrestle hold, or otherwise harass my children, Jonathan and Cole, it's "Uncle!" "Uncle who?" "Uncle Randy!" (my brother) that sets them free. They're already looking forward to the next generation being required to yell "Uncle Jonathan" and "Uncle Cole." Ah, tradition.

• *"I'll be a monkey's uncle!"* is used to express astonishment (which is why it has an exclamation mark), as in the following typical dialogue between Paul and Pam:

Paul: Hello, Pam. How are you?

Pam: I'm feeling pretty darned good, Paul. Say, isn't that a python tightening itself around your neck?

Paul (looking at himself in the mirror): Well, I'll be a monkey's uncle! That *is* a python tightening itself around my neck!

• To talk to someone "like a *Dutch uncle*" refers to lecturing someone bluntly and sternly. The opposite of Dutch uncle, one might suppose, is Portuguese aunt, which, in certain parts of Eastern Europe is used when lecturing someone gently while pouring port wine against the side of his or her head.

• *Bob's your uncle!* is a mostly British expression that means, according to *Chambers 21st Century Dictionary* (Cambridge University Press, 1996), "something should follow simply as a matter of course." The example given is: "Just flick the switch and bob's your uncle!" (Yes, lower case here.)

How did the word "uncle" get into these idioms without a written order from the attorney general? The expression "Uncle Tom" comes from a novel written long ago (see "Great Uncles of the Classics" in the next section). As for the others, the *Oxford Dictionary of Modern Slang* (Oxford University Press, 1992) hypothesizes that "cry uncle" may be an anglicization of the Irish *anacol* (mercy). Who knows? No one can say for sure where any of these expressions (except for Uncle Tom) comes from. After all, there's no evidence that Dutch uncles are any more stern or blunt than, say, Japanese uncles (although they do tend to be taller). Nor is there anything astonishing, when you think about it, about monkeys having uncles, unless those monkey uncles are fluent in Mandarin Chinese or able to play "Sgt. Pepper's Lonely Hearts Club Band" on the accordion.

Ultimately, the root of the majority of uncle expressions, as with most expressions of all kinds, "lie shrouded in the mists of time," says Richard Lederer, author of *The Word Circus* (Merriam-Webster, 1998) and other books on the peculiarities and perplexities of the English language.

Uncle Slang

As far as slang is concerned, you don't have nearly as many slang alternatives for the word "uncle" as you do with words like "sexual intercourse" and "obesity." Nevertheless, according to various slang thesauruses, you can refer to your uncle, if you so desire, as *Unc*, *Unk*, *Uncs*, *Unks*, *Nuncle*, *Nunks*, or *Nunky*. Of course, you may not wish to do so if old Unc is an English teacher or you risk getting hit (bashed, bammed, socked) over the head (bean, noggin, bonnet) with a slang thesaurus.

GREAT UNCLES OF THE CLASSICS (AND NEAR CLASSICS)

Old Uncle Tom, perhaps because he had a good PR agent, got his name and (in modern editions) his likeness on the cover of Harriet Beecher Stowe's world-famous novel, *Uncle Tom's Cabin*. Most other uncles of literature have had to content themselves with supporting roles. Here, in chronological order, are some of the uncles you're most likely to encounter in the world of literature.

Uncle Zeus (*The Iliad, The Odyssey,* other ancient classics). Before there was Bill Gates, there was Zeus, and he ruled the universe. Like many of the ancient

Greeks, Zeus came from a big family, and he had scores of little ones to whom he was Uncle Zeus. Given the loose morals of the day, however (there weren't even safeguards against pornography on the Internet), many who called Zeus "Uncle" could also call him "Daddy."

Uncle Claudius (*Hamlet*). There was something truly rotten in Denmark, and it was Hamlet's Uncle Claudius. Evil Claudius killed Hamlet's father, usurped the throne, and—to add insult to injury—married his sister-in-law, Hamlet's mother. All this happened whilst Hamlet was away at college, majoring in medieval kingdom administration. He returned home to learn the bitter truth from the ghost of his father. He then agonized over whether to kill his uncle, or kill himself, or what. A real downer, even by Shakespearean standards.

Uncle Scrooge (*A Christmas Carol*). The name Ebenezer Scrooge, even more than Donald Trump, has become synonymous with greed. Old Scrooge was the main character in Charles Dickens's 1843 Christmas classic. He was known as "partner" to old Jacob Marley; "boss from hell" to lowly grunt Bob Cratchit; and "Uncle Scrooge" to Fred, his sickeningly cheerful nephew. In the end, of course, old Uncle Scrooge was aided by three ghosts (Hamlet's father not among them). He saw the light, and on Christmas morning transformed into a generous, compassionate man, who only wanted to buy a big kosher turkey for Tiny Tim.

And who knows? If Dickens had written a sequel, Tiny Tim may eventually have come to address the reborn Ebenezer as "Uncle Scrooge."

Uncle Tom (*Uncle Tom's Cabin*). Published in 1852, the novel bearing the name of Uncle Tom's abode became an instantaneous best-seller both in the northern United States (it was banned in the Confederacy) and in Europe. With graphic images of the cruelty of slavery, the novel did more to end that toxic institution than anything else shy of Gettysburg. It is unclear whether old Tom had any blood nieces and nephews, but he was referred to as "Uncle Tom" by the young white "Mas'r" George. Incidentally, the Uncle Tom that appears in the novel was hardly servile. The Uncle Tom image, that of a black man who grovels before whites, is derived not from the book, but from years of shabby theatrical interpretations of the story.

Uncle Remus (*The Tales of Uncle Remus*). This was the fictional narrator of African-American folktales, put into writing by journalist Joel Chandler Harris and first appearing in serial form in the *Atlantic Constitution* in 1896. There are 263 tales in all, all collected from southern blacks and told in southern black dialect. Most of the wonderfully funny stories involve the cunning Brer Rabbit and how he outwitted larger animals like Brer Fox and Brer Bear. The best of Harris's tales have been updated and captured in the marvelous volume, *The Tales of Uncle Remus* (Dial Books, 1987), as told by Julius

Lester, with captivating illustrations by Jerry Pinkney. The tales are for uncles of any color to enjoy with their nieces and nephews.

Uncle Vanya (*Uncle Vanya*). This guy was a vodka-quaffing hypochondriac and hothead who played with guns. Yet he still got to play leading man in this famous play by Russian literary legend Anton Chekhov. Uncle Vanya first appeared on stage at the Moscow Art Theatre in 1899. The National Rifle Association is still trying to distance itself from old Uncle Vanya, and Charlton Heston steadfastly refuses to play the role.

Uncle Jim (*Portrait of the Artist as a Young Dog*). "I'll give her peaches! Peaches, peaches!" hollered Uncle Jim, in this book of autobiographical vignettes composed by Beat Generation poet Dylan Thomas. Thomas's Uncle Jim had a red face, a wet nose, and trembling, hairy hands. He smoked a pipe. He didn't show up for breakfast. His nephew Dylan's obscure verse makes other poets' obscure verse seem as clear as Wyoming air. (Although it isn't nearly as obscure as IRS form 1040-ES, Schedule C.) Peaches! Peaches, peaches! Dig, man?

Uncle Scrooge McDuck (*Donald Duck* and *Scrooge McDuck* comics). Cartoon legend Donald Duck has an uncle, Scrooge McDuck. This penny-pinching bird, a spin-off of the famous Dickens character, Ebenezer Scrooge, first appeared in comic book form in 1947. Uncle McDuck made his film debut in 1983 in the Disney cartoon classic *Mickey's Christmas Carol*. The character's voice, incidentally, was that of Allan "Rocky" Lane who also did the talking for Mr. Ed, TV's chattiest horse. McDuck, aside from his role as Donald's uncle, is still Duckburg's wealthiest and most miserly citizen. He spends much of his time hanging out in his vault, keeping tabs on his immeasurable wealth—much like real-life Disney chairman Michael Eisner.

Uncle Scrooge McDuck's nephew Donald, by the way, has three troublesome little nephews of his own—Huey, Dewey, and Louie.

Uncle Popeye (*Thimble Theater* and *Popeye the Sailor* comics). Not to be outdone by a dumb duck, Popeye, the spinach-swallowing cartoon sailorman, proudly boasts not three, but *four* mischievous nephews—Pipeye, Peepeye, Pupeye, and Poopeye. Uncle Popeye, of course, also had his own adopted "infink," cousin to the fiendish foursome—the mighty Li'l Sweet Pea.

Uncle Mickey (*Mickey Mouse* comic books, cartoons). No self-respecting American cartoon character, it seems, can be without at least a few nephews. Mickey, the world-famous Disney rodent has two—Morty and Ferdie Fieldmouse.

SAM THE MAN: A TALL GUY WITH STRIPED TROUSERS

Other than perhaps that big bald bird, Uncle Sam is the most common symbol used to represent the United States of America. No one knows quite where the guy originally came from, but he's been used as our national logo ever since the early 1800s. The Uncle Sam we know today—the tall, thin, stately gentleman dressed in a swallow-tailed coat with stars, striped pants, and a tricolor top hat—was drawn by James Montgomery Flagg, who served as his own model.

Who is Uncle Sam uncle to? Every one of us with a valid passport, presumably. But long before Flagg's Uncle Sam adorned all those recruiting posters, the old gent was often shown with his nephew, Brother Jonathan, generally depicted as a smart-alec kid with a big hat. In fact, for many years the two were used interchangeably as symbols of America.

Whatever happened to Brother Jonathan? Fascinatingly, he never really disappeared, but rather metamorphosed into a character indistinguishable from Uncle Sam himself, and so erased himself from history. In *Uncle Sam: The Man and the Legend* (Hill and Wang, 1959), Alton Ketchum wrote:

> *Many American cartoonists . . . favored Jonathan over Uncle Sam in the years before 1860. In general, those who worked in a lighter vein usually chose Jonathan, while more serious efforts involving the Government itself featured Uncle Sam. Physically, Jonathan was usually depicted as younger and more callow, though as time went on he grew to look more and more like Uncle Sam, who was never shown as other than a mature man.*

Why the United States Is Such a Great Country

Forget about those spacious skies and amber waves of grain. Forget about all the electric can openers, the Playboy Channel, the Elvis legacy, and Tater Tots. What really makes America great is our Uncle Sam. This chart objectively compares Uncle Sam to the national symbols of various comparatively puny countries, like England, France, Russia, Canada, and Japan, and proves beyond a doubt that the good old USA is the finest nation north of Equatorial Guinea—maybe in the whole world.

Symbol	Wears a Top Hat	Has Long White Hair	Sports a Beard	Career Potential with NBA
Uncle Sam	Yes	Yes	Yes	Yes
John Bull	No	No	No	No
Marianne	No	No	No	No
The Russian Bear	No	No	Yes	No
The Maple Leaf	No	No	No	No
The Rising Sun	No	No	No	No

UNCLE, SCHMUNKLE: WHAT THE HECK RHYMES WITH *UNCLE*?

Want to write a poem for Dad? Hey, no sweat. Lots of cool words rhyme with *dad* (fad, lad, Olympiad, Trinidad, Chad). For Mom we have a fair number of options, too (prom, Tom, CD-ROM, pompon). And for an aunt, aspiring poets have numerous prime alternatives (can't, rant, pant, slant, shan't). But if you want to write a poem about your uncle and you care whether it rhymes, you're stuck with the sorriest, most pathetic lot of words imaginable:

- Carbuncle (a pus-bearing inflammation of the skin, worse than a boil)
- Caruncle (an outgrowth of flesh)
- Peduncle (the base of a tumor)
- Truncal (who the hell knows?)

If you're really desperate for rhymes, or perhaps your uncle is a scoundrel, you can also throw into your poem some of the following choice selections (words that sort of rhyme with *uncle*):

- Dull
- Numskull
- Fool
- Ghoul
- Stool

No poet I, I passed along these words to a poet friend of mine, Jennifer Kane of State College, Pennsylvania, to see what she could do with them poetrywise. After her initial reaction (something akin to an emotional carbuncle), she tossed my list of miserable words into the recycling can and wrote a poem about uncles that doesn't rhyme. It's a beautiful poem nonetheless.

Uncle

Critical
Pivotal influence
With just a visit now and then . . .

Balancing out
And filling in
A branching family tree

My history

Of experience,
Broadened by your newness,
Your occasional
And special
Presence,

Your breath of fresh air
on which I would thrive,
Adoring your quirky mysteries.

The list of those
Who have shaped my life
Is full of the word—
Uncle.

JENNIFER KANE

Used by permission of the author, Jennifer Kane, ©1999.

HOW TO SAY "UNCLE"
AROUND THE WORLD

As good global citizens, it behooves us to know something of other peoples' tongues. To that end, today's language lesson brings us the word "uncle" as we encounter it around the world. This is not always an easy translation. In Japanese, for example, the word for uncle is *oji* if you're talking about your own uncle. It changes to *oji-san* if you're talking about someone else's uncle. In Arabic, and some other languages, the word will vary depending on whether you are talking about your mother's brother, your father's brother, or the husband of an aunt. In Korean, the brother of your father is *sham chun*, if he's unmarried. If the same uncle marries, you then would call him *jek un ahbuh gee*, which translates as "little father" and confers slightly greater status.

In the following languages, an uncle is an uncle is an uncle.

American English: *Uncle*
My uncle bites the heads off live chickens.

Bristish English: *Uncle*
My uncle bites the 'eads off live chickens.

Dutch: *Oom*
Mijn oom bij de kippen van levende koppen af.

Esperanto: *Onklo*
Mia onklo formordas la kapojn de vivantaj kokinoj.

French: *Oncle*
Mon oncle arrache la tête des poulets vivants.

German: *Onkel*
Mein Onkel beißt lebenden Hühnern den Kopf ab.

Norwegian: *Onkelen*
Onkelen min biter hodene av levende kyllinger.

Polish: *Wujek*
Mój wujek odgryza głowy żywym kurczakom.

Russian: Дядя
Мой дядя откусывает головы живым курам.

Spanish: *Tío*
Mi tío les arranca la cabeza con los dientes a los pollos vivos.

Turkish: *Amcam*
Amcam canli tavuklarin basini isirip koparir.

Quiz: Uncles of American History

Time to take out your #2 pencils and test your knowledge of uncles of the past.

1. True or False: President Theodore Roosevelt was uncle to President Franklin D. Roosevelt.

2. Which two past American presidents, as boys, were sent to live with wealthy uncles?

3. At the Battle of Little Bighorn (June 25, 1876), General Custer was defeated by Chief Crazy Horse and his Sioux Indians. After a tough winter, however, Crazy Horse was finally persuaded by his uncle to surrender. What was the name of Crazy Horse's uncle?

   a. Fearless Fox
   b. Spotted Tail
   c. Abe (Running River) Schwartz

4. Milton Berle, who began his career as a child comic and silent-screen actor, was the first star to gain national recognition in the pioneer days of television. He became known to millions of Americans as "Uncle Miltie." What was the name of his show?

5. Which famous brothers had a great vaudeville comedian named Al Shean for an uncle?

   a. The Marx Brothers
   b. The Wright Brothers
   c. The Flying Burrito Brothers

Answers:

1. False. Presidents Theodore and Franklin Roosevelt were distant cousins. FDR's wife, First Lady Eleanor, however, was the niece of Theodore Roosevelt. In fact, it was Uncle Teddy who gave Eleanor away to distant cousin Franklin on their wedding day.

2. The two lads who lived with wealthy uncles and went on to become presidents were Grover Cleveland and Herbert Hoover.

3. The answer is b. Crazy Horse's uncle was named Spotted Tail.

4. Milton Berle, or Uncle Miltie, hosted *The Texaco Star Theater*, which aired from 1948 through 1953. Berle, who had never been successful as a radio funnyman, also came to be known as "Mr. Television."

5. The answer is a. Writes Harpo Marx in his wonderful autobiography *Harpo Speaks* (Limelight Editions, 1961): "Once a month [circa 1900], Uncle Al came to visit, decked out in expensive flannels and broadcloth, matching fedora and spats, and ten-dollar shoes. He sparkled with rings and stickpins and glowed with the scent of cologne . . . as he got ready to go, Uncle Al would give each of us boys a brand-new dime." Uncle Al undoubtedly called nephew Harpo by his real name—Adolf.

Quiz: Famous Uncles of Today

Not all uncles—famous or otherwise—are dead, thank heavens. Here are a few questions about renowned uncles who are very much alive and kicking.

1. He may have directed *The Godfather*, but he is an uncle to actor Nicolas Cage.

   a. John Carpenter
   b. Francis Ford Coppola
   c. Federico Fellini

2. True or False: Bill Gates is the uncle of Macaulay Culkin, child star of such films as *Home Alone*.

3. Ruler of his country, king of his people, head of a large and extremely affluent family, this man's appointed governors consist largely of his many nephews.

   a. King Fahd Ibn Abdul Aziz Al Saud
   b. Nat "King" Cole
   c. B. B. King

4. If the next marriageable generation of Kennedys wind up procreating as freely as did their recent forebears, how many great and great-great nieces and nephews will Senator Edward M. (Teddy) Kennedy have if he lives to be as old as his mother, Rose?

   a. A figure approximately equal to Uncle Teddy's belt size multiplied by the number of syllables in Chappaquiddick.
   b. A number slightly less than the population of Massachusetts.
   c. Standing shoulder to shoulder, wearing penny loafers with no socks, they would stretch from Harvard Square to the tip of Cape Cod.

Answers:

1. The answer is b. Actually, Nicolas Cage's real name is Nicholas Coppola. Uncle Francis, director of numerous hit films, including *The Godfather* (1972), *The Godfather, Part II* (1974), and *Peggy Sue Got Married* (1986), also has a famous sister—actress Talia Shire.

2. False. While Macaulay Culkin played the role of the fabulously wealthy kid in the 1994 movie *Richie Rich*, and the character (especially if you put glasses on him) bears an uncanny resemblance to Microsoft monarch Bill Gates, Culkin and Gates are unrelated.

3. The answer is a. All fourteen emirates, or provinces, of Saudi Arabia are governed by King Fahd's brothers, sons, and nephews. Travel advisory: Don't plan on visiting the king and his governing brood in summertime; the average July temperature in Riyadh is 108°F.

4. The answer is b.

3

POP CULTURE UNCLES

The Nazis in World War II had spies who spoke English as well as any Wisconsin librarian. How could American soldiers discover whether a Shakespeare-quoting suspect was really raised in Boston or Berlin, Minneapolis or Munich? Easy. If he quoted Shakespeare, he was a German spy—no American GI would ever quote Shakespeare. Sometimes, however, to be doubly certain, the Americans would ask a suspect soldier a question about baseball, like who won the 1946 World

Series?* That was, of course, a trick question, because the war ended in 1945.

But the point is that we, as Americans, share a common cultural heritage, and that which doesn't come from baseball comes from television and movies. This is why names like Uncle Fester, Uncle Bill, and Uncle Buck are far better known to most Americans than the names of popes and presidents (but not baseball players). In this chapter we take a look at Fester, Bill, Buck, and the other great uncles of popular American culture.

UNCLES IN SITCOMS

Horrifying, but true: the average American watches about four hours of television daily. That means that our vision of reality is largely derived from the ultimate in fantasy—the boob tube. What then does the tube teach us about uncles? Well, as you'll see from the following look at uncles from television's most popular sitcoms, they are mostly single men, rather weird, and often grouchy. But they're also lovable.

Uncle Fester (*The Addams Family*, 1964–1966, ABC). Played by Jackie Coogan. They're creepy and kooky and all together ooky. But Fester, fun-loving uncle to Wednesday and Pugsley Addams of Cemetery Lane, amateur chemist, and explosives expert, is always up for

---

* The St. Louis Cardinals did.

a good fishing trip, using dynamite as bait. Hairless, with blackened eyes and lips, Elizabethan collar, and ever-present lightbulb in the mouth, Fester is as dashing as an uncle could be. (Do not confuse this Uncle Fester with the cyberdegenerate "Uncle Fester" who sells books on the Internet describing how to make methamphetamine in your own kitchen.)

Uncle Fester (2) (*The New Addams Family*, current, Fox). Played by Michael Roberds. Like all the characters in this updated version of the classic show, this newfangled Uncle Fester takes some getting used to. Once you do, you'll find that he's quite good, really. Yet watching this Fox-model Fester, you'll sometimes swear that he's Joe Besser of the Three Stooges in ghoulish disguise.

Uncle Joe (*Petticoat Junction*, 1963–1969, CBS). Played by Edgar Buchanan. What would life in Hooterville be like without old Joe Carson, Uncle Joe, moving kind of slow at the junction? Uncle Joe is involved in one failed money-making scheme after another, but he always has time to "manage" (swing on the porch of) the old Shady Rest Hotel, and keep an eye out for his three comely nieces, Billie Jo, Bobbie Jo, and Betty Jo. Whether they were all named after Uncle Joe remains one of Hooterville's most enduring mysteries.

Uncle Charley (*My Three Sons*, 1960–1972, CBS). Played by William Demarest. He is rough and tough and mean and crusty, but he has a heart of gold and is doing a first-rate job helping to raise Mike, Robbie, and Chip. Uncle Charley, when not chewing out one of the boys for wearing his hair too long, is playing the cello or looking as macho as a man can look wearing an apron and carrying a spatula.

Uncle Bill (*Family Affair*, 1966–1971, CBS). Played by Brian Keith. When their parents are killed in a car crash, Buffy, Jody, and Cissy are taken in by their uncle, international jet-setter Bill Davis. The kids are often glum because Uncle Bill is away on business, but what can he do? The man must work hard to afford that swank New York apartment. In any case, Mr. French, the British butler and nanny, provides quality care while Uncle Bill is zipping across time zones.

Uncle Martin (*My Favorite Martian*, 1963–1966, CBS). Played by Ray Walston. *Los Angeles Sun* reporter Tim O'Hara finds a crashed UFO, from which steps a professor of anthropology from Mars whose area of expertise is the primitive planet Earth. The Martian can't get his spacecraft working and is forced to remain Earthbound. Making the best of things, he befriends the reporter and adopts the guise of Martin O'Hara, Tim's uncle. Uncle Martin can be awfully cocky and arrogant at times, even by Martian standards, but it's evident that his attachment to his fake nephew eventually becomes most real.

Uncle Martin (*The Patty Duke Show*, 1963–1966, ABC). Played by William Schallert. It originally ran concurrently with *My Favorite Martian*, but *The Patty Duke Show* also features an Uncle Martin. This one isn't from Mars, but from Brooklyn Heights. This Uncle Martin heads a household that features identical cousins—that's right, identical cousins—Patty and Cathy Lane. Patty is the daffy American-born-and-bred daughter. Cathy is the warm and sensitive European niece. Uncle Martin is wise and loving and wonderful, as a father and uncle of identical cousins should be.

Uncle Herman (*The Munsters*, 1964–1966, CBS). Played by Fred Gwynne. Not to be out-ooked by those Addamses, the Munsters of 1313 Mockingbird Lane are headed by Frankenstein–look-alike Herman Munster, funeral worker and kind uncle to niece Marilyn. Poor Marilyn, pretty and normal, can't find a guy to ask her out twice. Uncle Herman is sympathetic, but unwittingly continues to frighten away all suitors.

Uncle Jed (*The Beverly Hillbillies*, 1962–1971, CBS). Played by Buddy Ebsen. Jed Clampett was a poor mountaineer barely kept his family fed, until one day, when shooting for some food, up through the ground come a-bubbling crude—oil that is, black gold, Texas tea. The next thing you know, Uncle Jed's a millionaire, and he moves to Beverly Hills where he hopes to find gainful employment for his nephew, Jethro Bodine. He fails at that, but Uncle Jed is still a source of much homespun wisdom, a model of thrift, and a dashing character in his floppy brown hat.

TV Uncles: A Comparative Analysis

Which TV uncle is your favorite? Don't have one? Let this chart help
you decide.

	Married	Gainfully Employed	Rich	Has Antennae	Spooky	Irritable
Uncle Fester	No	No	No	No	Yes	No
Uncle Jed	No	No	Yes	No	No	No
Uncle Martin (from Mars)	No	Yes	No	Yes	No	Yes
Uncle Martin (from Brooklyn)	Yes	Yes	No	No	No	No
Uncle Joe	No	No	No	No	No	No
Uncle Charley	No	Yes	No	No	No	Yes
Uncle Herman	Yes	Yes	No	No	Yes	No
Uncle Bill	No	Yes	Yes	No	No	No
Uncle Leo	No	No	No	No	No	Yes

Uncle Jesse (*The Dukes of Hazzard*, 1979–1985, CBS).
Played by Denver Pyle. He drove a beat-up old pickup
truck with a gun rack, and he was forever saving the
day for those good old boys and high-speed motorists
Bo and Luke. Jesse was a fine uncle, by redneck or
other standards.

Uncle Leo (*Seinfeld*, 1989–1998, NBC). Played by Len
Lesser. When he isn't shoplifting in bookstores, Uncle
Leo is busy keeping tabs on nephew Jerry so that he can

file regular reports to Jerry's parents in Florida. Uncle Leo has a few interesting psychological nits, including the belief that Nazis lurk around every corner of New York City. Uncle Leo's biggest concern in life, after dodging Nazis, seems to be that Jerry say hello to him. Of course, Jerry keeps forgetting to do this, which is always enough to shatter Uncle Leo's spirits.

THE MAN FROM U.N.C.L.E.

On NBC prime time from 1964 through 1968, millions of Americans tuned into the adventures of secret agents Napoleon Solo (Robert Vaughn) and Illya Kuryakin (David McCallum). The suave, sophisticated, and always nattily dressed agents worked for that international organization of aging Boy Scouts— U.N.C.L.E.

Agents Solo and Kuryakin took on fascist war criminals, evil dictators, and other assorted bad guys, but their biggest and baddest adversary was THRUSH, a secret society of international thugs who were to organized crime what Wal-Mart is to retailing. Regardless of the bad guy of the week, Solo's and Kuryakin's lives were constantly in danger. Despite this, they always had something incredibly glib to say, and Solo always managed to chase at least one skirt.

Throughout the show, U.N.C.L.E. was never referred to as anything other than U.N.C.L.E. What did it stand for? Observant viewers found their answer in only one place: coyly buried in the credits at the end of each show. "We wish to thank the United Network Command for Law Enforcement without whose assistance this program would not be possible" was one of the last items to scroll across the television screen. This little wink to the viewer's intelligence was one of the small things that made *U.N.C.L.E.* such an incredibly cool show and a tribute to uncles everywhere.

The 1966 spin-off show, however, *The Girl from U.N.C.L.E.*, starring Stefanie Powers as female agent (get this) April Dancer, was an embarrassment not only to uncles, Powers, and NBC, but even to the idiotic medium of television. At times, *The Girl* could make *Three's Company* look intelligent. Unlike *Three's Company*, however, which defied ratings gravity for years, *The Girl* sank into oblivion after one suffering season.

UNCLES OF SONG

Popular songs that feature uncles are few and far between. For some reason, however, three of the great rockers of the sixties and seventies produced fine songs about uncles. None won any awards for great lyrics, but they are all highly whistleable tunes.

Uncle John ("Uncle John's Band," The Grateful Dead). Let's see. He has a band, and they play to the tide, and you can come and hear them by the riverside, and maybe you'll see Uncle John come to take his children home. That's about all we know of the elusive yet musically talented Uncle John. We don't know what riverside he plays by, or whether he plays to high or low tide, or whose children he takes home. Perhaps someday science will provide the answers.

Uncle Ernie ("Fiddle About," The Who). A wicked man. Terribly sick. When little Tommy's parents go out on a date, Uncle Ernie is asked to come and baby-sit. Big mistake. Poor Tommy, born without the ability to see or hear, is only marginally aware of what goes on around him. Uncle Ernie takes advantage to play sadistic games. And where are the social workers from family services? Off playing pinball, no doubt.

Uncle Albert ("Uncle Albert/Admiral Halsey," Paul and Linda McCartney). Why are we so very sorry? Because the kettle's on the boil? Big deal. So what? Is there a reason we haven't heard a bloody thing all day? Is the phone out of order? Has anyone checked E-mail? No, of course not. There's no one left at home. What exactly is a "butterpie," anyway, and how much saturated fat and cholesterol is in the average serving?

Although no songs about uncles of any note have been recorded in the past several years, there has been a veritable explosion in the number of musical groups named after uncles. Here is a sampling of some of those groups. None have quite reached superstar status, but perhaps in time. . . . The description of each group comes directly from its promotional material, unedited.

My Gay Uncle. "A punk ska and occasionally hip-hop alternative band from the suburban porta potty of Mahwah, New Jersey."

Uncle Dave and the Tall Guys. "A Connecticut based band with an interesting blend of hardcore and upbeat punk influences."

Uncle Dirt Nap. "Swamp rock band from Washington."

Uncle No. "From Macedonia, Ohio. An up and coming quartet of musicians whose style, somewhere between hardcore and funk, is extremely popular today."

Uncle Heavy and the Seeing-Eye Horns. "Seven-piece musical group featuring original music and unique cover material. Latest release: 'You're Soaking in It.'"

Uncle Hoy. "A big, fat sextet. Their songs reflect a deep familiarity with the roots of R & B, yet their sound is shmushed from a wide variety of bananas."

Uncle Knucklefunk. No description available.

Uncle $am Band. "In 1997 released their first full CD called 'Love in a Blender.' Their songs take real life moments and capture the feelings."

Uncle Tupelo. "This band from Belleville, Illinois, epitomizes country/rock, country/punk, insurgent punk, whatever you want to call it."

RADIO'S INFAMOUS UNCLE DON

He was born Howard Rice, changed his name to Don Carney, and was known to American radio listeners as "Uncle Don." Every night from 6:00 to 6:30 on WOR radio in New York, children in eighteen states could tune into Uncle Don's show, which ran from September 1929 through February 1949.

Here is how the show began:

> *Hello, little friends, hello*
> *Hello nephews, nieces, mine*
> *I'm glad to see you look so fine . . .*
> *I've many, many things to tell you, on the radio*
> *This is Uncle Don, your Uncle Don*

Uncle Don would read the funnies, tell stories, sing songs, and hold talent contests. But he was more than just another pretty voice. He formed the Uncle Don Institute of Child Guidance and Recreation, a non-profit group that battled child delinquency and boredom. He also set new standards for radio by becoming the first show host to personally check out sponsors and their products before accepting them for the program. He was one of the most respected people on radio, beloved by zillions of tots, and an honor to unclehood.

And then . . . it happened.

One night, so the story goes, he was ending his program and, thinking he was off the air, said, "I guess that'll hold the little bastards." And that incredible blooper marked the swift end of Uncle Don's career. I remember hearing this story from my parents when I was a young boy growing up in New York. I've heard the story several times since from various sources. It's a neat story. There's only one problem—it is apparently untrue.

"None of it is true, even though you can find people today who swear they heard it. . . . It simply never happened," write radio historians Frank Buxton and Bill Owen in their book, *The Big Broadcast 1920–1950* (Viking Press, 1972). "A columnist in Baltimore, where Uncle Don was not heard, made up the story to fill space on an otherwise dull news day. And the story just grew and grew."

UNCLES OF THE MOVIES

Some of the silver screen's finest performances have been of uncles. No uncle performance, alas, has yet to win an Academy Award for best actor—although Paul Newman came darned close with a nomination for his portrayal of Uncle Hud in the movie *Hud*, and the French movie *Mon Oncle* (*My Uncle*) did win the award for Best Foreign Film. Here is how uncles have been depicted on the silver screen over the years. As you'll see, we generally fare better than we do on television, but still, you find a good number of boozers and losers.

Uncle Hud (*Hud*, 1963). Played masterfully by Paul Newman. Hud Bannon, uncle to Lon Bannon, drives a pink Cadillac through the Far West, sleeps with married women, and drinks like there's no tomorrow. He is wild, arrogant, and irresponsible. All the same, young, impressionable Lon looks up to Uncle Hud the Stud. When the family comes into a crisis, however, Hud's immorality and self-centeredness proves too much even for the adoring nephew. Lon decides that Hud is really a big jerk, and he drives off into the sunset, leaving his bemused uncle in a cloud of dust and steer droppings.

Uncle Buck (*Uncle Buck*, 1989). Played by John Candy. The quintessential bachelor must watch over his two nieces, Tia and Maizy, and nephew Miles in their plush suburban home. He doesn't know what to do. He burns the toast. Beats up the clothes dryer. Feeds blue toilet water to the dog. But love overcomes ineptitude, and he turns out to be a pretty good uncle after all.

Uncle Albert (*Mary Poppins*, 1964). Played by Ed Wynn. He loves to laugh and can't stop laughing, no matter how hard he tries, no matter how hard his oh-so-sensible niece Mary Poppins tries to make him stop. Unfortunately, when Uncle Albert laughs, he also rises to the ceiling. Oh well. Mary Poppins, always knowing what to do, simply joins him for a spot of uplifting tea.

Uncle Eddie (*National Lampoon's Christmas Vacation*, 1989). Played by Randy Quaid. Uncle Eddie turns the belch, sidewalk urination, and the crotch scratch into pure art. The guy is high class all the way, from his hunting cap turned sideways, to his stained white T-shirt, down to his threadbare slippers. What a role model he is for those Griswold kids, Rusty and Audrey!

Uncle Fester (*The Addams Family*, 1991; *Addams Family Values*, 1993). The same character as in the old television show (see "Uncles in Sitcoms"), this time artfully and ghoulishly played by Christopher Lloyd. Sexy Uncle Fester is the leading man in both Addams movies. In the first, an impostor takes his place in the Addams household; in the second, a tart schemes to marry him for his money. Regardless of his travails, Uncle Fester is always ready to romp and stomp with nephew Pugsley and niece Wednesday.

Uncle Martin (*My Favorite Martian*, 1999). Christopher Lloyd is at it again, this time not as the terrestrial oddball Uncle Fester, but as the otherworldly oddball Uncle Martin. He looks flashy in his all-silver talking spacesuit, and his super Martian powers and ultrasarcastic attitude serve to turn newfound nephew Tim's world upside down.

Uncle Henry (*The Wizard of Oz*, 1939). Played by Charley Grapewin. Dorothy's Uncle Henry plays a very minor role in this genuine American classic about a tornado, a pair of ruby slippers, and makeshift wizardry. Why? What were the producers trying to hide from us? Was Uncle Henry possibly cheating on Auntie Em with that neighbor lady on the bicycle? Was he growing something illegal behind the barn? Was he hiring illegal aliens to work his fields, dressing them as tinmen, lions, and scarecrows to deceive the immigration authorities?

Uncle Owen (*Star Wars*, 1977). Played by Phil Brown. Luke Skywalker wants to run off and join the Imperial Academy. Owen Lars, Luke's guardian uncle, something of a hick, just wants his nephew to stay home on the desert planet of Tatooine and work the moisture farm. Uncle Owen gets fried by agents of the Evil Empire. Obi Wan Kenobi then becomes an uncle figure to Luke and helps guide him to intergalactic greatness. Some hard-core *Star Wars* fans hold that Uncle Owen wasn't really Luke's blood uncle, but was in fact Obi Wan Kenobi's brother.

Uncle Hulot (*Mon Oncle*, 1958). Played by Jacques Tati. Young Gerard lives in a crazy house with a big silver fountain that looks like a pregnant sardine. Mom and Dad and the gal next door are garish, superficial, and cold. Thank goodness there is Uncle Hulot. He can't hold a job. He isn't much of a ladies' man. And he wreaks havoc on the big sardine. But Hulot is a good man, a kind man, a friend to his nephew Gerard, and, in the end, winds up teaching a thing or two about kid relations to Gerard's all-business dad. Winner of the Oscar for Best Foreign Film, *Mon Oncle* portrays unclehood at its funniest and fishiest.

Uncle Lon (*The Asphalt Jungle*, 1950). Played by Louis Calhern. A sultry Marilyn Monroe calls him Uncle Lon, but he isn't her true uncle. It's a discredit to the word. "Uncle" Lon, with his pencil-thin mustache and rakish style, is actually her sugar daddy, a bad card player, and a double-crossing crook.

Uncle Scar (*The Lion King*, 1994). Voice of Jeremy Irons. Evil, conniving Uncle Scar kills his brother, the king, and grabs the throne. If that weren't bad enough, he refers to his nephew Simba as the "little hairball." Not since Cruella De Vil plotted to skin 101 dalmations have the creators at Disney served up such an unscrupulous cartoon figure. Why did they have to make him an uncle, huh? We should all boycott Disney for this outrageous slight to unclehood.

Uncle Lex (*Superman IV: The Quest for Peace*, 1987). Played by Gene Hackman. Superman's nemesis Lex Luthor teams up with his young nephew Lenny (Jon Cryer) to foil the Man of Steel once and for all. Lex may be the world's foremost criminal, but he is far from the world's foremost uncle. He is condescending and rude to his nephew, calling him, among other things, the "Dutch Elm disease of the family tree" and a "pathetic product of the public school system." Of course, truth, justice, and the American way reign supreme in the end, and Uncle Lex winds up wearing well-deserved stripes.

Uncle Bill (*Never Give a Sucker an Even Break*, 1941). In his last starring role, W. C. Fields plays Uncle Bill to Gloria Jean, the charming and feisty young singer/actress making her way through Hollywood. There's a movie within a movie here, and both are mishmashes of sight gags and silly one-liners. But throughout the hubbub, Uncle Bill, with his crimson nose, mumbled wisecracks, and whiskey breath, is clearly the fermented object of his niece's affection. The final words of the movie (after

W. C. picks himself up from a car wreck): "My Uncle Bill—I love him!"

Uncle Paulie (*Rocky, Rocky II, Rocky III*, etc.). Played by Burt Young. Paulie, brother to Adrian, brother-in-law to Rocky, uncle to Rocky Jr., has the intelligence of a grub, the social consciousness of a turnip, and the charisma of wood glue. He smokes fat cigars, breaks people's fingers, and eventually blows all of the Rock's boxing money on speculative investments. Paulie's only redeeming quality seems to be his affection for his nephew, Rocky Jr. (Rocky Krakoff). In *Rocky IV* (1985), for example, Uncle Paulie takes time out of his busy loafing schedule to teach the Pebble how to read racing forms.

Uncle Joe Shannon (*Uncle Joe Shannon*, 1978). Played (and written) by Burt Young. He figured his role as an uncle in *Rocky* did his career good, so why not try it again? Sad, sad. This story of a down-and-out trumpet player makes for one bad movie. Still, *Uncle Joe Shannon* is not the worst movie of all time.* It is not, for example, nearly as bad as the movie *Dune*. (I'm pretty certain that there was some kind of uncle featured in *Dune*, but the movie is just too painful to think about, much less write about. Let's just skip it.)

---

* The worst movie of all time is *A Stranger Among Us* (1992), in which Melanie Griffith—believe it or not—plays a "tough" New York City cop. If that isn't absurd enough, the squeaky-voiced blond then goes undercover as a Hasidic Jew. This is arguably Hollywood's worst casting since John Wayne played Genghis Kahn in the 1956 megaflop *The Conqueror*. Thank goodness no uncles were featured in either of those two disasters.

A Thoughtful Critique of Movie Uncles

Which uncle role deserves our biggest applause, and which deserves our tartest raspberries? Use the following chart to compare and decide. Also, consider the message that Hollywood sends us about uncles. You may want to write a letter.

	Married	Gainfully Employed	Reckless	Handsome	Drinks Beer and Belches	Has a Pot-Belly
Uncle Buck	No	No	Yes	No	Yes	Yes
Uncle Albert	No	No	Yes	No	No	No
Uncle Paulie	No	No	Yes	No	Yes	Yes
Uncle Eddie	Yes	No	Yes	No	Yes	Yes
Uncle Hud	No	Yes	Yes	Yes	Yes	No
Uncle Henry	Yes	Yes	No	No	No	No
Uncle Lex	No	No	Yes	No	No	No

Quiz: Uncles of Popular Culture

Time to get serious and test your knowledge of famous uncle characters.

1. In *The Man from U.N.C.L.E.*, where was the secret entrance to U.N.C.L.E. headquarters?

    a. Ian's Fish-n-chips, on Piccadilly Square, London
    b. Del Floria's tailor shop, somewhere in the east 40s of New York City
    c. Joey Buttafuoco's Auto Body Shop in Baldwin, Long Island

2. *The Girl from U.N.C.L.E.* was played by actress Stefanie Powers. What was her real name?

    a. Sallie-Mae Plowers
    b. Stefanie Zofja Federkievicz
    c. Abby Schwartz

3. Which famous television uncle was played by the same guy who, as a child star, appeared as the insufferably cute kid in Charlie Chaplin's 1920 movie *The Kid*?

    a. Uncle Jed (Buddy Ebsen)
    b. Uncle Martin (Ray Walston)
    c. Uncle Fester (Jackie Coogan)

4. In the game of Monopoly, what is the name of the dapper little gentleman with the white mustache, tuxedo, top hat, and cigar who appears on the Chance and Community Chest cards?

    a. Uncle Pennybags
    b. Uncle Tycoon
    c. Uncle Bigbucks

5. As an occasional guest star on *Bewitched*, this actor played the forever snide Arthur, Samantha's uncle. In a great fluke of fate, this actor also once took on the role of Uncle Herman's doctor on *The Munsters*. He even provided the voice for Templeton, the crafty barn rat in the great kids' movie *Charlotte's Web*.

   a. Dick Van Dyke
   b. Jackie Gleason
   c. Paul Lynde

6. As a guest star on *Petticoat Junction*, this actor played the visiting Uncle George, whose cultured charms and worldly ways wound up making Uncle Joe feel jealous and irate.

   a. Ronald Reagan
   b. Don Ameche
   c. Dean Martin

Answers: 1. b; 2. b; 3. c; 4. a (His first name is Rich, and his office, naturally enough, is in Atlantic City.); 5. c; 6. b

Quiz: Can You Match the Uncle?

Let's see how much you have really paid attention to your television and movie watching over the years. Match the preferred pastime or choice characteristic with the appropriate TV or movie uncle below.

1. Frequently consulted his crystal ball.

2. Owned the Davis and Gaynor Construction Company.

3. Stood six foot, seven inches in stocking feet and had a wife named Lily.

4. Served on a U.S. Navy ship as a cook.

5. Said, "Earth's all right for a visit, but I wouldn't want to live there."

6. Had to fend off advances from the impassioned woman across the street.

7. Had a droopy-eared hunting dog named Duke.

8. Was rarely, if ever, seen without a bow tie and cardigan.

9. On film, drove a convertible down dusty roads well beyond the speed limit; in real life, sells pretzels, lemonade, and spaghetti sauce.

a. Uncle Bill

b. Uncle Joe

c. Uncle Herman

d. Uncle Fester

e. Uncle Charlie

f. Uncle Jed

g. Uncle Martin

h. Uncle Buck

i. Uncle Hud

Answers: 1. d; 2. a; 3. c; 4. e; 5. g; 6. h; 7. f; 8. b; 9. i

4

UNCLES OF COMMERCE

America is a land not only of mom-and-pop businesses, but of aunt-and-uncle ones as well. Aunt Jemima, of course, is a leading supplier of pancakes and pancake goo. Aunt Millie's spaghetti sauce has covered pasta dishes and stained white shirts from coast to coast. And we mustn't forget the distinguished Uncle Ben.

We start this chapter with a hard look at Uncle Ben, the godhead of quick rice, the potentate of pudding, the prince of pilaf. We will then turn our eyes to a sampling of the thousands of American entrepreneurs who are using the name "uncle" in their pursuit of after-tax profits.

UNCLE BEN: THE PUZZLING
PRINCE OF PILAF

As far as commercial icons are concerned, stately look-ing Uncle Ben is right up there with Mrs. Paul, Colonel Sanders, and the Pillsbury Doughboy. But who really knows anything about this man who advocates quick rice at every meal?

He was, according to official company documents, a rice farmer in old Houston, "known for producing a quality product." That's all we have, folks. All the devoted rice-eating public is ever told of Uncle Ben is what you just read. But when did he live? Whose uncle was he? Is the guy you see on the box the real Uncle Ben or some guy from a Los Angeles modeling agency? Has he considered Rogaine? Over a dozen extremely polite requests on the author's part to get that infor-mation from Uncle Ben's, Inc., a division of Mars, Inc., were rebuffed. Why?

Is it possible that the family of Uncle Ben is due millions in royalties for the use of the old man's image, and the Mars executives are trying to escape their legal and moral obligations? Could matters be even worse?

Might Uncle Ben be a prisoner in Mars corporate headquarters, forced to dress up and pose for pictures while subsisting on microwaved rice, Three Musketeers bars, and tap water?

The official Uncle Ben's company history, available through the corporation's promotional website (www.uselessinformation.com), barely mentions Uncle Ben. Instead, there's a dreadfully dim story about these two business types having dinner at their favorite Chicago restaurant, and one guy (a real wit) turns to the other and says, "I'm determined to bring to the American consumer the same high-quality rice served to the armed forces during World War II."

Odd conversation. Odder yet is that I've known many men (including a number of uncles of mine) who served in the armed forces during World War II, and I don't recall a single one ever saying, "Oh yeah, that little clash with Hitler sure was hell, but all the blood and gore was worth it for that yummy GI-issue rice that awaited us at chow call!"

UNCLE ENTREPRENEURS

Why would anyone call his business Uncle Ernie's, as does Ernest Lowy, who just happens to run one of the finest bakeries in eastern Pennsylvania? I asked Ernie, and this is what he said:

> *It was my son's idea. He's my partner in the business. I was gonna call the place Lowy's, but he thought that was boring. We have these friends of ours whose children have called me "uncle" their whole lives. One day, Kim walked in and called me Uncle Ernie, and my son said, "That's it! Let's call the business Uncle Ernie's! You're a big, robust, jolly kind of guy. Wouldn't it be nice if everyone had an Uncle Ernie who baked cookies for them?" And ever since then, we've called the business Uncle Ernie's.*

If you happen to be in the area, especially if accompanied by your nephews and nieces, stop by and try one of Uncle Ernie's fabulous black-and-white cookies. Uncle Ernie's is located at 1444 Linden Street in Bethlehem.

Other uncle businesses in my area include Uncle Vito's Pizzeria at 149 W. Nesqeuehoning Street in Easton, which offers a truly fine, crusty pizza. Here is what owner Vito Campanelli had to say about naming the restaurant:

> *Actually, I didn't name it; my five-year-old nephew, Antonio, named it. We were sitting around one day, and my brother turned to little Antonio and asked him what we should name the new business. He said we should call it Uncle Vito's, so that's what we called it.*

When asked why he calls his used-furniture business at 501 North 10th Street in Allentown Uncle Ron's, owner Ron Wirth responded:

We have a large family, and I have seven nieces and seven nephews, so they all call me Uncle Ron. But that's what everybody calls me! I had white hair and a white beard when I was quite young, and that made me look like an uncle. As for the business, there never was much question what I'd call it. Now, even when customers I talk with on the phone get to meet me, they often tell me that they're glad to finally meet their Uncle Ron.

In addition to these businesses, our country is blessed with other small uncle businesses, far too numerous to list here. But here's a taste of some of the more interesting sounding ones, real-life businesses handpicked from assorted and sundry Yellow Pages. I'm not personally familiar with these concerns, but judging by their fine names, I'd say they're certainly worthy of your esteemed patronage, possibly even a plane ticket to get to them:

Uncle Salty's Tropical Fish
31656 S. Coast Highway
Laguna Niguel, California 92677

Uncle Milt's Meat Market
6235 E. 14th Ave.
Denver, Colorado 80220

Uncle Joe's Rolling Zoo & Ponyrides
5261 Cambell Rd.
Mobile, Alabama 35661

Uncle Andy's Granola Factory
269 S. Mountain Rd.
Gardiner, New York 12525

Uncle Sneedley's Toy Shop
135 Cleveland Ave.
Loveland, Colorado 80537

Uncle Bob's Popcorn
1147 N. Columbus Blvd.
Tuscon, Arizona 85712

Uncle Moe's Burritos
14 W. 19th St.
New York, New York 10011

Uncle Louie's Street Wise Kid (martial arts studio)
19201 Parthenia St.
Northridge, California 91324

Uncle Jack's Saw Shop (chainsaws)
Steadman Rd.
Mayville, New York 14757

Uncle Credit Union
2100 Las Paritas Ct.
Livermore, California 94550

Uncle Bob's Propane
2433 Middle Country Rd.
South Setauket, New York 11720

Uncle Punk's Pizza
921 N. Alma School Rd.
Chandler, Arizona 85224

Uncle Phil's Tonsorial Parlor (barbershop)
128 Pulaski Blvd.
Kings Park, New York 11754

TRULY OFFBEAT UNCLE BUSINESSES

The World Wide Web lists a growing number of uncle companies doing business in cyberspace, many of which are rather boring—pornography, semiautomatic guns, that sort of thing. But it also has two listings that catch the eye: Uncle Jim's Worm Farm and Uncle Milton Ant Farms.

Uncle Jim's Worm Farm (http://www.unclejim. com). "Now let's face it! You probably aren't your average guy or gal if you are interested in buying worms wholesale," says Uncle Jim on his spiffy website. You can say that again, Jimbo. There are, unfortunately, no pictures of worms on the site, but there are some wonderful tidbits of worm trivia. Bet you didn't know, for instance, that worm excrement is eleven times richer in potash than the average yard's topsoil.

Uncle Milton Ant Farms (http://www.ant-farm. com). Uncle Milton claims to have shipped over a billion ants in his forty years of business. If that isn't enough to give Milton's wife a serious case of the heebie-jeebies, consider this: in Africa, the combined weight of all the ants would be more than that of all the elephants. Only an uncle would know such trivia! Uncle Milton, by the way, only ships ants on Mondays so they don't die at the post office over the weekend. Smart guy.

5

KIDS ON UNCLES

Who's better to say what's great about uncles than real-life nieces and nephews? Featured in this chapter are the fervent opinions of about fifty of them. Roughly half belong to the bright and spirited students that make up Mrs. (Tara) Tobin's fifth-grade class at the Parkway Manor School in Allentown, Pennsylvania. The remainder belong to the two dozen teenagers I found on several occasions hanging around the Lehigh Valley (Pennsylvania) Mall, usually wolfing down Big Macs and fries as they spoke.

WHAT MAKES FOR A
FAVORITE UNCLE?

The nephews and nieces were asked to name their very favorite or most important uncle or uncles, and explain why they picked who they did. Here are some of their responses.

Teenagers at the Mall

"My favorite uncle is my Uncle Jeff, my mom's brother. I don't get to see him much because he lives in England, but he calls us on holidays and makes every effort to get together with us whenever he can. Last time we visited him, like a year ago, he got so drunk that he fell off of a second-story balcony and had us scared to death that he was really hurt. Then he got up laughing like crazy, and started running all around the house in his underwear."

SARA, 16

"I like my Uncle Harold, my mom's brother. He's a cop and just a real helpful guy. Whenever our family is in trouble or needs him, he's there. Like when we had to move, he helped us move."

AMBER, 15

"My great-Uncle Zello, my grandmother's brother, was very special to me. He was always someone I could talk to, because he was so laid-back and

*warm. And he never tattled on me. I could tell him
anything and not have to worry about it getting
back to my parents. Once I wanted a little kitten
sooo bad, and I remember being on the front porch
of our house begging my mother. It was Uncle Zello
who talked her into letting me have it."*

BROOKE, 17

*"I really like my Uncle Bob, my mom's brother.
He's really into sports, and we often go over to
his house to watch the games on his fifty-six-
inch TV."*

SETH, 18

*"My Uncle Ed, my father's brother, is the best. He
lives in Denver, halfway across the country, so I
only get to see him about twice a year. But we
always have lots of fun. When me and my family
went out there last summer, he took us to the
movies, to malls, and even to Rocky Mountain
National Park. Even when all we did was stay at
his house, I still had a good time. He's just such a
happy, friendly guy."*

KENNY, 15

*"My Uncle Jeff, my dad's brother, is really cool.
He let me take his Lexus to the prom."*

ADAM, 17

*"My Uncle Francis is my favorite uncle because
I can relate to him. He can be like a real kid*

sometimes, like when he tells jokes—really, really
stupid jokes. Also, he enjoys a lot of the same stuff
that I do, like soccer.

LAURENT, 14

"I like my Uncle Mark, my dad's brother. He
makes me laugh. On his wedding day, he got
drunk as a skunk, sucked in the helium from
the balloons, and talked like one of the
Munchkins."

MELISSA, 16

"Favorite uncle? Can't say. I've got four of them—
and they're all great guys!"

SAMANTHA, 16

Fifth Graders (Ten Years Old, More or Less)

"My Uncle Larry is my favorite because he says I
am just as special to him as his own daughter—if
he had one."

SHELBY

"My Uncle Ivan is my favorite uncle because he is
the funniest person I know."

DAVID

"My favorite uncle is my mom's brother. He plays PacMan with me."

JUSTIN

"My favorite uncle is Uncle Michael because he taught me golf, and he is really nice and funny. He also picks me up and throws me in the pool."

BEN

"My favorite uncle is Uncle Arthur because he is very athletic, so we can play sports together such as soccer, running, and football."

GRAHAM

"My favorite uncle is my youngest uncle on my dad's side. That is because he has no kids yet, so me and my brother are the center of attention."

EMILY

"Uncle Michael is my favorite because he talks to me a lot more than my other uncle."

BRITTANY

"My favorite uncle is Uncle Jeremy, on my mom's side, because his apartment is across the street from the playground. Also because he's cool!"

AMANDA

"My Uncle Larry, because he does not smoke and he is not an alcoholic. He is also very enjoyable and fun to play with."

DANIELLE

THE TOP TEN DREAM OUTINGS WITH UNCLE

The young ones were asked, "If you could take a day off and do anything you wanted or go anywhere you wanted in the whole world with your favorite uncle, where would you go?" Here are their answers—with number one being the most dreamy.

Teenagers at the Mall

1. Cruise Mall of America
2. Spend the day at the world's biggest amusement park
3. Go skydiving
4. See a professional football game
5. Hike through a tropical rain forest
6. Do Paris
7. Ride go-carts
8. Go horseback riding in the woods
9. Take a Caribbean cruise
10. Spend a day rolling dice in Vegas

Fifth Graders

1. Go to a great, big amusement park with water rides
2. Go jet skiing or waterskiing
3. See a professional hockey game
4. Go parasailing
5. Go snowboarding
6. Visit the zoo
7. Play the very latest video games
8. Try scuba diving
9. Go to a big-league baseball game
10. Chuck around a football in the park

THE TOP TEN MOST-OFTEN-CITED OUTINGS FROM HELL

Here the boys and girls were asked, "What's the last thing on Earth you'd want your uncle to take you to do on a day off from school?" Here's what they said—with number one being the most hellish.

Teenagers at the Mall

1. Visit his dorky buddies
2. Gift-shop for his wife or girlfriend
3. Take a trip to the hardware store
4. Work on his car

5. Go golfing, with me as his caddy
6. Attend a Wayne Newton concert
7. Go to his office, so I can do gopher work
8. Visit the nursery to buy stuff for his lawn and shrubs
9. Attend a Yanni concert
10. Go early-morning fishing, using bloodworms as bait

Fifth Graders

1. Go on an eight-hour car ride, listening to his oldies tapes
2. Sit in his den and watch The Weather Channel
3. Visit a boring museum filled with stuff from the Renaissance
4. Go to see a *Sesame Street* or Barney play
5. Show him my schoolwork and have him correct it
6. Clean out his sock and underwear drawers
7. Play the "Quiet Game"
8. Watch him shoot pool
9. Pick up my friends and tell stories of cute things I did when I was a little kid
10. Pick up his friends and tell stories of cute things I did when I was a little kid

THE TOP TEN FANTASY UNCLES

The youngsters were asked, "If you could have anyone in the whole world, living or dead, real or make-believe, as your uncle, who would it be?" Number one was the most fantastic.

Teenagers at the Mall

1. Robin Williams
2. Bill Cosby
3. Moses
4. Tim Allen
5. Sean Connery
6. Bill Murray
7. Ghandi
8. Arnold Schwarzenegger
9. Kunta Kinte
10. Jack Nicholson

Fifth Graders

1. An uncle I already have
2. Michael Jordan
3. James Bond
4. Ty Warner (president of Ty Corp., creator of Beanie Babies)
5. Homer Simpson
6. Mickey Mantle
7. Uncle Fester
8. Bill Gates
9. Jerry Seinfeld
10. Albert Einstein

THE TEN CREEPS WE DEFINITELY WOULDN'T WANT AS OUR UNCLE

And the final question asked of the boys and girls was, "Who would be the last person on earth, alive or dead, real or make-believe, you'd choose to have as your uncle?"—with number one being the creepiest.

Teenagers at the Mall

1. Adolf Hitler
2. Saddam Hussein*
3. Ivan the Terrible
4. The Unabomber
5. Charles Manson
6. Bruce Willis (because he allegedly cheated on Demi)
7. Ebenezer Scrooge
8. The Menendez Brothers
9. Jack the Ripper
10. Howard Stern

* There is some irony that Saddam Hussein appears so high on our list. At age ten, Saddam (his first name translates to "he who confronts") left home to live with his uncle, Khairullah Tulfah. Uncle Khairullah, author of such fervent works as *Three Whom God Should Not Have Created: Persians, Jews, and Flies*, was said to be an enormous influence on the budding Iraqi leader.

Fifth Graders

1. Barney (the purple dinosaur, not Barney Rubble or Fife)
2. One of the Hansons
3. Jerry Springer
4. Mike Tyson
5. Marilyn Manson
6. Any of the guys on *Baywatch*
7. Ken (Barbie's boyfriend with the plastic hair)
8. Ozzy Ozborn
9. Scar from *The Lion King*
10. The man who does the Spaghetti-Os commercials, and says, "Uh oh, Spaghetti-Os"

6

AN UNCLING PRIMER

There may well come a time when the phone will ring in the middle of the night. Your sister or brother will have some kind of emergency, like maybe a nose that got stuck in an electric pencil sharpener, necessitating a trip to the hospital. Someone will be needed to watch the children, and you're it. Uncle Buck.

Especially if, like old Buck Russell, you're childless, this situation may give you a great deal of anxiety. That's normal. Before I had two of my own adorable little urchins, had I ever received a phone call from my sister asking me to watch her kids, I would have had a quadruple stroke. Fortunately, the little ones were living a thousand miles from me, so that never came to pass. Since the birth of my own children, I've watched over my niece and nephews a good number of times. Piece of cake. Honest.

The opportunity—yes, opportunity!—to watch your nieces and nephews is a blessing in heavy disguise. Trust me. If you were going to start a business, you'd want to work for other people first to get hands-on experience and make your mistakes with someone else's money, not yours. The same goes for kid care. Treasure those opportunities to practice on your sibling's children. But, of course, you don't want to practice too roughly. That's why I've put together the following guide to everything you need to know about taking care of little ones.

THE ABCs OF KID CARE FOR UNCLES

Okay, uncles. Here's what you have to know to be a responsible, respectable temporary guardian to those pint-sized nephews and nieces. Commit these points to memory and you can't go wrong. Well, not very wrong. For your convenience, it's all been properly alphabetized.

Aggggrrrrrrhhhhhh! Don't panic. Really. It's not that bad. Be glad you're not living in the old days, when your sister or brother might have had nine or ten children. Breathe deeply. Remember that you were once a kid yourself. You can relate. Do you have a dog at home? Essentially, kid care and dog care aren't that different. You feed. You clean. You provide comfort. Kids don't attract quite as many fleas.

Babies. Well, okay, panic just a little. Babies are work. They are crying-pooping-peeing-puking-eating machines. But they're also awfully cute. Favorite baby/uncle activity: bring your head down close, shake it wildly from side to side, let your cheeks and lips flap, and make bu-bu-bu sounds. Don't worry about spitting on the kid—he'll return the serve, and you may get a nice volley going.

Crying. This is Nature's way of dealing with hurt. After a minor injury or a frustration, children cry. After a good cry, they feel better. Give a crying child your attention. Show her you care. Allow tears to flow. Maybe say something like, "Ouch! Scratching your leg must have hurt. I understand why you're upset. I'd cry too!" Do *not* say, as some unthinking big people do, "Shhhhhh, shhhhh, shhhhh. Stop crying." That's not terribly comforting.

Diapers, changing. The key is to do it fast, sliding or rolling the youngster from old diaper to new, avoiding carpet stains, sludge-filled belly buttons, and sticky fingers. You also want to safeguard your face from a frontal fluid attack. That means keeping your nose at least five inches from the geyser when changing a girl, twelve inches for a boy. Don't worry about getting the diaper on perfectly. This isn't a fine art you're performing. The kid will rip the thing off in a few minutes anyway.

Exhaustion. Don't force children to sleep, lull them. Turn down the lights. Read *Goodnight Moon*. Sing songs, but no Jimi Hendrix. Try lullabies, such as my special version of "Hush, Li'l Baby": "Hush, li'l baby, don't say a word, Uncle's gonna buy you a mockin' bird. . . ." If that doesn't work, start recounting your life story. It puts your dates to sleep, doesn't it?

Freezer. Kids four through eighteen are amazed to see cold-blooded animals (fish, snails, insects) frozen and brought "back to life." Your Martha Stewart–like sister also will find immeasurable joy finding snails in her ice tray. Warning: dogs and cats are not cold-blooded. *See also* Marshmallows.

Gum. If you have, say, a six-year-old nephew or niece who is driving you batty with question after question after question (But *why* is an elephant bigger than an ant? But *why* is it raining? But *why* can't I go naked to services?), give him or her gum—like six wads of it. Have six more ready if needed. If you have two children firing questions at you, get them to play the who-can-be-quiet-the-longest game.

Hydraulics. *See* Diapers, changing.

Insults. Whatever the youngsters call you or do to you, the parents get it worse. Don't take it personally. Children will hate you one minute, adore you the next.

Jitters. Kids get them, too. On far less caffeine than it takes you. If you don't want to be watching over wired little hellions bouncing off walls, then be aware that many soft drinks contain caffeine. A glass of Mountain Dew, for example, has fifty-four milligrams of caffeine, about as much as half a cup of coffee. Most colas have something like thirty to forty-six milligrams. Always check the can or bottle. Remember that you can't go wrong with milk or water.

Kilts. Yes, men in Scotland wear skirts. (But don't use the word "skirt" around any Scotsmen or you risk having a caber tossed in your direction.) Try to break whatever rigid sexual stereotypes you grew up with. They're not healthy for either sex. You may find that your nieces gravitate toward playing house, and your nephews only want to play cops and bond brokers. That's okay, but let everyone know that all options are open and perfectly fine.

Lunch. Not to worry. Kids will eat almost anything as long as it's prepared by an adult other than a parent, even if it's the same dish the parents have tried to serve unsuccessfully. It's part of the nature of the beast. Use it to your advantage.

Marshmallows. Freeze before serving. For sandwich purposes (*see* Quick meals), use only the real thing, not "marshmallow spread," which lacks the right chewability.

Noises in the night. Children can fear many things for many reasons. Most children at some time become fearful of monsters and ghosts that lurk in the darkness. Don't tease. Don't ignore. Listen. Comfort. Explain. Empower. Encourage laughter. Say, "There are no monsters here. But even if there were, you are big and strong, and you could push those monsters and make them cry." Then pretend to be a toothsome monster (baby carrots make great fangs), encourage your nephew or niece to push you, and react with big crocodile tears.

Oriental carpets. Roll them up when you first get the kids home. Your job will be tough enough without having to worry about spilled chocolate milk. Put away the crystal. Remove sharp objects, toxic materials (toilet-bowl cleaner, pesticides), and medications (including supplements that contain iron) from kids' reach. With everything put away, relax. Have fun.

Peanut butter. They look alike. They smell alike. They have the same ingredients (peanuts, sugar, vegetable oil). But for some reason, the generic brand tastes like putty. Don't get cheap with peanut butter. Buy only the best. One peanut butter caveat: don't ever give a child peanut butter on a spoon. It's too big a choking hazard. The gooey goop is meant to be served atop bread or crackers or mixed into cookies and muffins, not eaten straight.

Quick meals. Take two slabs of bread. Smear with peanut butter. Slice one banana lengthwise and lay on top of peanut butter. Add four frozen marshmallows. Voilà. Dinner is served. In the kids' eyes, you'll be a world-class chef.

Rough play. Don't limit it to nephews. Nieces love wrestling, too. Make sure you let them win. Being a kid is tough—always being told what to do and when to do it, and being smaller than everyone else. Naturally, they love it when they can beat up their big uncle. Be dramatic. Say, "Pleeeeze, pleeeeze, let me up!"

Sweets. Three kinds—preferred, backup, and desperation.

- Preferred: Anything chocolate; gummies, especially if they're in the shape of something disgusting, like a roach; red licorice sticks; cookies with chips; ice cream cones with sprinkles; birthday cake; cotton candy; Pez, especially cherry; tiny wax bottles filled with "juice;" miniature jellybeans; red Jell-O
- Backup (eaten only when preferred options aren't available): Cookies with fruit filling; candied apples; black licorice sticks; shortbread; candy corn; saltwater taffy; low-fat frozen yogurt, no sprinkles; big jellybeans; green or yellow Jell-O

- Desperation (eaten only when nothing else sugary is in sight): White gumdrops that taste of clove; sourballs; Jordan almonds; fruit pie; nonfat gingersnaps; red and white after-dinner mints; Tic Tacs

By the way, sugar may rot teeth and provide empty calories, but it does not cause hyperactivity in kids, okay? That's a myth. Scientists have studied the matter to death. What they've found is that, if anything, sugary treats (after the initial excitement of seeing them) are more likely to sedate children than rile them up. Sugar when mixed with caffeine, however, is another story altogether.

Tickling. A tiny bit of rib poking may be okay, but too much tickling, like past the point when the child objects (even if she's still laughing), is dreadfully obnoxious. It makes the child feel powerless. No good.

Unpleasant odors. After you've checked the garbage, the oil furnace, the basement, the attic, and you've called the local environmental agency, check the kid's pants. Next time, you'll know where to start. (*See* Diapers.) By the way, don't ever ask a child if he's poopie and expect the truth. They're not programmed that way.

Vanishing children. On outings, tell your nephews and nieces who to approach in case they get lost. (Traditionally we've been told children should approach a police officer or salesperson, but some security experts now say a mom with kids is the safest bet.) Make sure the little ones know their address and phone number; if they're too young to remember this data, slip a piece of paper into a pocket with the essential information.

Wine. Tempting. Tempting to sedate a wild child with a glass of cheap muscatel. Don't. Alcohol endangers the health of the infant brain.

Xerox. Bored with board games, the sandbox, and watching Disney videos? Take the kids into your office. Have them photostat their hands and various other parts of their anatomy. The tots will be ecstatic! Don't let them look into the light of the machine. And hope the boss doesn't walk in.

Yelling. You won't need to, much. As a rule of thumb, kids are much better behaved around other adults than they are around their own parents. This is because they live with their parents, and they know that Mommy and Daddy may be crazy at times, but they're no axe murderers. You're not one either—but the children don't know that for sure. So don't yell when they're acting horribly, just give them your best psychopathic evil eye. If you don't know how, see Robert De Niro in *Cape Fear* or any of the raptors in *Jurassic Park*.

Zippers. A child won't catch a cold going out into the chilly night. Got that? Ask any doctor—the only way you catch a cold is by coming into contact with an infected person's viruses. So discourage your nieces and nephews from shaking hands with anyone who sniffles, and make sure they wash before mealtime. But where it comes to dress, let the child's comfort be your guide.

THE SUPREME CHALLENGE OF SIMULTANEOUS UNCLING AND FATHERING

For those of you who already have children of your own, unless you're one of those chauvinistic relics of the past who leaves all childrearing to your (resentful, beleaguered) wife, you presumably know something about how to handle children. For you, the supreme challenge won't be diapering, or feeding, or bathing, but rather how to keep the cousins from killing each other.

Step 1:
Remove All Lethal Weapons from the Play Area

This includes the obvious—guns, knives, hammers, cattle prods, swords, bows and arrows, mace, slingshots, clubs, bats, darts, and hammers. But it also includes the not-so-obvious—shoelaces, hangers, tomato stakes, scissors, staple guns, cans of Raid, statuettes, and thick rubber bands.

Step 2:
Get Ready to Negotiate the Peace

Rivalry among cousins isn't all that different from sibling rivalry, and sometimes it's just as intense. I've seen a fair share of cousin-clashes myself, mostly between my son Clay and my nephew Clancy (both six). They generally revolve around toys—who had which toy first. I can't say that as the adult in charge I've ever been terribly adept at soothing ruffled cousin feathers, so I took this chapter as an opportunity to learn something new. I thought it appropriate to call my own first cousin, Robert Jaffe, Ph.D., a successful psychotherapist in Encino, California, to get his advice. (He is eight years my senior, so we never fought over toys.)

Cousin Dr. Jaffe told me that arguments between cousins or siblings generally revolve around the yearning for attention, or are an attempt to gain power or ownership (of, for example, a toy). Here are some of his suggestions for handling warring cousins:

• Don't compare. A child who feels he or she isn't as good as another isn't motivated to try harder. Instead, the child tends to feel like the situation is hopeless. So never say, "Why can't you be as nice as your cousin?" Comparisons intensify rivalries and make situations worse.

• Don't encourage contests. They also intensify conflict.

• Set rules. Let the kids know what is okay with you and what isn't. For example, you might say, "Don't hit or push. That behavior is *not* all right with me." Or, "Don't call names. It hurts people's feelings and I don't approve of that."

• Reinforce cooperation. Catch the cousins "being good" and playing nicely, and praise them for it. Be specific. Say things like, "It's so nice seeing you all playing so well together. It really makes me want to visit more often." If the kids do fight, treat them as a unit. Don't be the judge and jury to determine who is guilty.

• Keep them busy. Help the cousins find fun activities. Bored children are more likely to fight. Either do something with them, or help them get started on something. Above all, show them an adult who loves them and is glad to be visiting.

• Model calm. We all react to other people's energy. Kids are especially sensitive to the energy shifts and moods of others. If the cousins are fighting like cats and dogs, give yourself a quick sniff. Are you in a combative mood? If so, you yourself may be fueling the fire.

The second-biggest challenge you'll have watching over your nephews and nieces and your own children will be finding the energy and patience to give them all your attention. Most impatience and exhaustion around kids, I find, is caused by mental drifting. Instead of really connecting and being there with the tykes, we're worrying about the chores that need tending around the office and home. Try not to drift. Take the time you spend with little ones and make it truly all theirs. Be there mentally as well as physically. Chores can wait.

CAPITALIZING ON YOUR UNCLE STATUS TO MEET ATTRACTIVE WOMEN

For those of you uncles without children or a wife, pay heed to the following tale.

A year ago, my then-five-year-old son and I went out for lunch together. We were at this funky restaurant (owned and operated by a chiropractor) off the side of the main road. It was a beautiful day, and we were out on the patio. Clay decided to climb a tall concrete fountain. I asked him to come down. He ignored me. I asked again. He ignored me. I took him around the waist and pulled him down. He reared back and slugged me in the face.

I put him down on solid ground, held him firmly by the shoulders, and told him very sternly, "You are *not* to ever hit me in the face again." He started to cry.

I hugged him and told him I loved him, but that my loving him did not mean that I would allow him to maul me. When I looked up I noticed two women sitting at the next table, watching. One was looking me in the face. "I feel like crying," she said, "that was sooo beautiful. You were loving but firm, just the way a man should be with a child." And then she gave me that eye, the kind of eye that women usually reserve for Brad Pitt or Leonardo DiCaprio.

Most women get all gushy inside when they see a man interacting well with kids. They can't help it. This is a deep instinctual thing, undoubtedly seeded in a woman's evolutionary drive to procreate. When she sees a man who is good with children (even if he's with his own kid and presumably married), her unconscious brain sees a potentially good mate for herself, and she will turn goopy.

Listen up, single uncles: Nothing, but nothing— not a custom-made suit, or a Harvard degree, or a fourteen-karat timepiece, or your ability to cry through *Fried Green Tomatoes*—will impress women more than seeing you interact lovingly with your adoring nephews and nieces.

7

THE ULTIMATE
FUNHOG UNCLE

my great-Uncle Davey died when I was just five years old. Still, I remember him. For he was the quintessential funhog uncle. Whenever the family got together, even before he had his coat off . . . whoop, Uncle Davey would heave me up on his square shoulders and run me around, making loud fire truck sounds. I felt like I was riding atop the world. And that is exactly what uncling should be about. So. This chapter, written to help uncles make little ones feel atop the world, is dedicated to my Uncle Davey.

A WORLD OF AMUSEMENTS

Don't think you need to take your nieces and nephews
to Disneyland and blow your entire paycheck in order
to give them a screaming good time. There are oodles
and oodles of ways to thoroughly delight children right
around the house, or within a foam football's throw.
Try a few of the activities suggested here.

Knock-Knock Jokes

Most children love them. They're eminently silly. Easy
to remember. Easy to repeat. Here are a handful of
knock-knocks to get you started.

> Knock-knock.
> > *Who's there?*
> Adam.
> > *Adam who?*
> Adam my way—I'm coming in!

> Knock-knock.
> > *Who's there?*
> Anita.
> > *Anita who?*
> Anita rest!

> Knock-knock.
> > *Who's there?*
> Armstrong.

Armstrong who?
Armstrong as an ox—and you have the
brain of one.

Knock-knock.
Who's there?
Cain.
Cain who?
Cain you hear me? Knock-Knock!

Knock-knock.
Who's there?
Cashew.
Cashew who?
Cashew see I'm busy?

Knock-knock.
Who's there?
Wayne.
Wayne who?
Wayne, Wayne, go away, come again another day!

Knock-knock.
Who's there?
Dozen.
Dozen who?
Dozen matter to me!

Knock-knock.
Who's there?

Zinc.
Zinc who?
Zinc or swim!*

Magic Tricks

Why was *Home Alone* such a big hit with kids? Because children love seeing another child playing tricks on adults. Teach your nieces and nephews a few magic tricks to play on their parents, and you'll never be forgotten. The classic disappearing-coin box, which can be purchased in any magic shop and many toy stores for about $2, can be handled adeptly by a five-year-old. So can the classic ball-and-vase, disappearing scarf, or change-the-penny-into-a-dime trick.

Here's a trick that requires no special gadgets at all. Have your niece or nephew hand you a crayon behind your back. Without looking at the crayon, tell exactly what color it is! The secret: swing your empty hand in front of you as you point to your niece and say, correctly, "The color is orange!" What she doesn't see is that you've used the crayon to mark your thumbnail. (To help reduce the chance of detection, as soon as you've looked at the marking, wipe it off with your index finger.)

Dozens upon dozens of other tricks can be learned by taking a trip to your local library or bookstore, and grabbing a book such as one of the following:

* Used with permission of Sterling Publishing, Co., Inc., 387 Park Avenue S., New York, New York 10016 from *Zany Knock Knocks* by Rodney M. Cole, text © 1993 by Ronny M. Cole, illustrations © 1993 by Rich Garramone.

• *Blackstone's Secrets of Magic*, by Harry Blackstone. A classic by a legend. First published 1929. The most recent version, a $7.00 paperback, is published by Melvin Powers Wilshire Book Company of Hollywood, California.

• *Blackstone's Tricks Anyone Can Do*, by Harry Blackstone. This is my favorite for its utter simplicity. The latest version (1996) is an $8.95 paperback published by Citadel Press of Secaucus, New Jersey.

• *The Magic of Micah Lasher*, by Micah Lasher, is a big, well-illustrated guide to easy tricks. It's a great book, although it doesn't offer as many ruses as the Blackstone volumes. Available in paperback through Fireside (1996) for $15.00.

Excellent Readings

Books can be a blast. And you can be the one to show your nieces and nephews just what a blast they can be.

Public libraries are one of this nation's best uses of tax dollars—take advantage by hanging out in one with your nieces and nephews. Any library will have a special kids' section, and many will have a special kids' librarian. Ask her for recommendations. She may have some favorites of her own, or she may hand you printouts of recommended reading lists. My local library has numerous such lists, including some very specialized ones, like books that teach right from wrong, books that promote certain religious values, and books that tout multicultural harmony. My library also has a few entire books about children's books, such as *Books Kids Will Sit Still For* by Judy Freeman (R. R. Bowker, 1990), which gives minireviews of 2,184 books for tots. (Ms. Freeman must be a riot at cocktail parties.)

It's not a bad idea to have a mini kids' library in your home for when the nieces and nephews come to visit. Children's books, like children's clothes, are quickly outgrown, so don't spend a fortune. Check out flea markets, garage sales, street vendors, and discount catalogs for the cheapest reads.

As a rough rule of thumb, for any nephew or niece you're likely to read to (under age seven or eight), if you like a book, he or she won't. And vice versa. Above all, kids love repetitiveness and predictability in their literature. They love phrases that get repeated over and over and over and over again. It makes them feel clairvoyant. Have your niece or nephew "read" the phrase out loud with you each time it comes up. And make sure to wave your arms around a lot as you read any exciting sections. Youngsters love exaggerated gestures—but make certain not to smack anyone in the nose.

Go Fly a Kite

I'm not talking here about your typical stupid flimsy plastic $2.99 Spiderman kite from the discount store. No sir. Any uncle can fly a stupid flimsy plastic $2.99 Spiderman kite from the discount store. You are the

Ultimate Funhog Uncle! For you, nothing will do but an eleven-foot jet-black toothy shark, made of durable nylon taffeta on fiberglass spars. It costs $36.50 (not including string), but, man, is it worth it!

The "Sky Shark" is available through Into the Wind, a company at 1408 Pearl Street in Boulder, Colorado, 80302-5307. They specialize in kites and kite equipment, and they'll be happy to send you a catalog if you call their toll-free number: 1-800-541-0314. In addition to the big carnivorous fish, you'll find humongous kites that look like frogs, cats, bats, birds, and fish, and even one that looks like a UFO. And if you really get into kite flying, you can subscribe to *Kite* magazine, a quarterly published by American Kite Company, 13355 Grass Valley Avenue, Grass Valley, California 95945. A one-year subscription (four issues) is $14.00. You may find yourself flying kites even when the nieces and nephews aren't around.

Throw a Boomerang

Boomerangs are tons of fun, nieces and nephews love them, and they're much easier to throw than many uncles think . . . once you know the secret to a successful return.

1. Find a large, open space.

2. Face into the wind.

3. Turn to three o'clock if you're right-handed, nine o'clock if you're left-handed.

4. Grasp the boomerang between the thumb and first two fingers. It doesn't matter whether you grab the shorter or longer arm, just make sure that the flat (usually the undecorated) side is facing away from you.

5. Hold the boomerang straight up and down or at a slight angle, but never horizontally. The best angle will depend on the design of your particular boomerang and on wind conditions, so experiment. You want to throw it overarm, like a baseball—*not* sidearm, like a Frisbee! Aim at the horizon, and snap your wrist, letting the boomerang spin out of your hand.

6. It should fly in a big circle and come back to you. Catch it by clapping it between the palms of your hands as it hovers downward.

7. Give your nieces and nephews a chance! Most children five and older can get the hang of it.

The Into the Wind catalog (see "Go Fly a Kite") offers a fair selection of boomerangs. Many toy and hobby shops stock them, too. Or, if you're a Web surfer, check out http://www.boomerangs.org/where.html. You'll find listings of lots of boomerang vendors, as well as connections to an unbelievable number of other boomerangs-related sites.

Find a Fair

Most fairs take place in the summer and fall. Keep an eye out in your local paper. Call the local chamber of commerce. Or dial 1-800-555-1212 and ask for the toll-free numbers to the tourism bureaus for your state and any nearby states. Most larger cities have such an office, too. Call and ask about special-event calendars. Some cities and states even have special literature packets on fairs, carnivals, and other kid-friendly seasonal activities.

Visit a Museum

The same tourism people can tell you whether there are special children's museums in any particular area. I've taken Gregory and Stephen to Philadelphia's Franklin Institute, a science museum for children (215-448-1200), and we had a great time running up and down the two-story human heart. I've also taken Clancy and Clayton to the Museum of Natural History at the Smithsonian Institution in Washington (202-357-2700). The Smithsonian is perhaps the best museum in the world—and it's free! Unfortunately, my nephew and my son were only three the time we went, and they spent more time picking up gum wrappers than they did looking at all the exhibits. (We'll have to return again soon, now that they're older.)

For listings of really cool museums that the tourism people might not tell you about, see *America's Strangest Museums* by Sandra Gurvis (Citadel, 1998) or *Offbeat Museums* by Saul Rubin (Santa Monica Press, 1997). Your nephews and nieces would definitely enjoy the Cockroach Hall of Fame in Plano, Texas; the Voodoo Museum in New Orleans; the Rattlesnake Museum in Albuquerque; the Tooth Fairy Museum in Deerfield,

Illinois; or The Teddy Bear Museum in Naples, Florida.
And what niece or nephew could possibly resist the
Toilet Seat Art Museum in San Antonio; Mister Ed's
Elephant Museum outside of Gettysburg, Pennsylvania;
or The Museum of Pez Memorabilia in Burlington,
California?

Sing a Song

Some of the best times I've had with my nephews and
my children have been spent singing songs. We ad-lib
quite a bit. Kids love to hear their names incorporated
into songs. Whenever I get together with Gregory and
Stephen, for instance, we're always up for a few good
verses of the following silly little ditty, which takes on
various forms, depending on how goofy we feel on a
particular day:

Untitled (Sung to the tune of "The Toreador Song" from *Carmen*)

Greg, chicken leg, eating apple pie
Took a big hunk of it
Shoved it in Stephen's eye
Stephen said, "Oh, my, my
Greg, you got to try this,
This is wonderful pie!"

Sometimes we're up for something a little more traditional, like "I've Been Working on the Railroad" or
"Clementine."

I've Been Working on the Railroad

I've been working on the railroad all the livelong day
I've been working on the railroad just to pass the time away
Can't you hear the whistle blowin'? Rise up so early in the
     morn
Can't you hear the captain shoutin',
(Gregory) *"Dinah, blow your horn!"*
(Gregory) *Dinah won't you blow* (3×) *your horn* (repeat)

(Stephen) *Someone's in the kitchen with Dinah*
Someone's in the kitchen I kno-o-o-w
(Stephen) *Someone's in the kitchen with Dinah*
Strummin' on the old banjo

Clementine

In a cavern, in a canyon, excavating for a mine
Dwelt a miner, forty-niner, and his daughter Clementine

(Refrain)
Oh my darling, oh my darling, oh my darling Clementine
You are lost and gone forever, dreadful sorry, Clementine

Light she was and like a fairy and her shoes were number
     nine
Herring boxes without topses, sandals were for Clementine

Drove she ducklings to the water every morning just at nine
Stubbed her toe against a splinter, fell into the foaming
     brine

Ruby lips above the water, blowing bubbles soft and fine
But alas! I was no swimmer, so I lost my Clementine

In a churchyard near the canyon where the myrtle doth
*   entwine*
There grow roses and other posies, fertilized by Clementine

Then the miner, forty-niner, soon began to peak and pine
Though he oughter jine his daughter, now he's with
*   Clementine*

In my dreams she still doth haunt me, robed in garments
*   soaked in brine*
Tho' in life I used to hug her, now she's dead I draw
*   the line*

Now ye Boy Scouts, heed this warning to this tragic
*   tale of mine*
Artificial respiration would have saved my Clementine

How I missed her, how I missed her, how I missed my
*   Clementine*
Till I kissed her little sister and forgot my Clementine

If you'd like the lyrics to twelve hundred other
songs, from the Beatles to Raffi and Broadway show
hits to traditional French lullabies, I heartily recommend picking up a copy of *Rise Up Singing*, a 280-page
book that not only has it all, lyricwise, but also gives
you the chords and features a truly amazing set of

indexes. You can look up songs by their titles, by their artists, by subject (America, ecology, friendship, spirituals, work), or even by their cultural background (English, German, Hebrew, Irish, Spanish, etc.). The book can be ordered directly through the publisher for $17.95 plus $5.00 shipping. Contact Sing Out!, P.O. Box 5253, Bethlehem, PA 18015-0253. Toll-free ordering number: 1-888-SING-OUT.

Unfortunately, there is one song not included in the aforementioned book that any self-respecting uncle should know. Just in case you don't, here are the lyrics:

The Gopher Guts Song

Great green gobs of juicy grimy gopher guts
Mutilated monkey's feet
Itsy bitsy squashed up teeth

Ten-quart can of all-purpose porpoise pus
Dipped in pink lemonade

Tell a Scary Story

Why wait till Halloween? You think ghosts and ghouls don't work in the off-season? Kids expect scary stories from their uncles. It's a time-honored tradition. Don't have any spine-tingling tales to tell? Check out the *Scary Stories for Sleep-Overs* paperback series from Lowell House Juvenile. *Scary Stories for Sleep-Overs*, *More Scary Stories for Sleep-Overs*, and *Still More Scary Stories for*

Sleep-Overs are available in bookstores or you can call the company directly at 1-800-323-4900. Or, if you think the kids can handle it, go to the Master of Disaster himself: Edgar Allan Poe. His "The Tell-Tale Heart"—after 150 years—is still guaranteed to dry your mouth and put sweat on your forehead. (Question on "The Tell-Tale Heart": could the old man with the one pale blue eye possibly be an uncle?!)

GOING TO THE MOVIES

The first time I ever went to the movies as an adult accompanying a child was the time I took my "little brother" (with the Big Brother/Big Sister program) Herminio to see Bruce Willis in *The Last Boy Scout*. It was 1991. Herminio was about ten and small for his age. I was about thirty-five—old enough to know better. I hadn't even glanced at a movie rating since I had turned eighteen! After all, I didn't yet have children of my own or a niece or nephew to consider. So I never gave the ratings a moment's thought. And as a result, there we were, little Herminio and his "big brother"—allegedly a positive influence in his life—sitting in a theater in a small town where people know one another, watching a movie with language that would make even a sailor blush and graphic violence galore. (I don't remember if there was graphic sex, too, but there probably was.) After the movie, I got some accusatory looks from the people in the lobby. It was embarrassing.

Don't make the mistake I did! Understand something about the ratings. The following chart will help you.

Film Ratings Made Easy for Uncles

Rating: G

Official Motion Picture Association of America definition: General audiences. All ages admitted.

What it really means: What difference does it make? G films come around only about once a century, and they only play in Kansas.

Rating: PG

Official Motion Picture Association of America definition: Parental guidance suggested. Some material may not be suitable for children.

What it really means: They won't see anything worse than most of what's available on television, and nothing nearly as bad as Jerry Springer.

Rating: PG-13

Official Motion Picture Association of America definition: Parents strongly cautioned. Some material may be inappropriate for children under 13.

What it really means: Movie offers sex and violence comparable to your average video game. You may not want to tell the parents that you took their kid to see this.

Rating: R

Official Motion Picture Association of America definition: Restricted. Under 17 requires accompanying parent or adult guardian.

What it really means: You definitely don't want to tell the parents that you took their kid to see this. Your niece or nephew may have to explain certain scenes to you.

Rating: NC-17

Official Motion Picture Association of America definition: No children under 17 admitted. Age limit may vary in certain areas.

What it really means: On your nephew's seventeenth birthday, take him to see his first NC-17 movie. Hey, what are uncles for? (Let an aunt take your niece.)

DINING OUT, KID-STYLE

Candlelight, crystal wine glasses, soft music, fine food . . . yeah, right. There's only one kind of place where kids fit in perfectly at mealtime, but most zoos close at six. That being the case, and you not having any peanut butter in your cupboards, you might just have to take them out to a restaurant. Ah, but where? Here's a quick rundown of the restaurants that your nieces and nephews are most likely to ask you to take them to.

McDonald's. The world's largest purveyor of dead cows, which are Mcground, Mcsalted, Mcbagged, Mcdouble-bagged, Mcboxed, and served to you by a minimum-wage worker who sorely looks like she needs a break today. *Highlights for the kids*: Telling their friends they went to McDonald's with their uncle; a big play area, a good place for nephews and nieces to push smaller children around, possibly hurt one, and instigate a Mclawsuit.

Burger King. My nephews and I call it "Booger King," which is not necessarily an insult, although it certainly could be interpreted that way. It all depends on the intonation, which changes depending on how long the Whoppers have been sitting out before we bite into them. *Highlight for the kids*: Junky little plastic toys, the perfect size for clogging toilets.

Taco Bell. We call it "Taco Smell," which doesn't mean that those refried beans with cheese don't touch our hearts—in more ways than one. Note that the "hot" sauce and the "mild" sauce are exactly the same. *Highlight for the kids*: Squeezing the little sauce packets out all over their uncle's white shirt and tie.

Pizza Hut. We call it "Pizza Slut," which is by no means any reflection on the fact that independent pizza parlors make far better pies and charge considerably less. Of course, you can also get pasta at Pizza Hut. If you do, be sure to tell your nieces and nephews about the Pizza Hut billboard in Stone Mountain, Georgia, where locals reported an apparition of Jesus in a forkful of spaghetti.* *Highlight for the kids*: It's fun to blow their noses in the salad bar.

KFC. Colonel Sanders's Kentucky Fried Chicken, that is. We'd like it better if it were "Uncle Sanders." "Colonel" is so macho, so aristocratic, so militaristic. *Highlights for the kids*: Throwing the little leaden rolls around the dining area; pretending to be the Colonel by sticking wet napkins to their chins and saying, "Ya'll better duck if ya'll don't want your eye taken out by one of dese here rolls."

---

* The story of the remarkable billboard is told in *Way Stations to Heaven: 50 Sites Across America Where You Can Experience The Miraculous* by Sandra Gurvis (Macmillan, 1996). Writes Gurvis in description of the billboard: "Held aloft by a fork and nestled among the spaghetti, sauce, and oregano were a crown of thorns, two deep-set eyes, a nose, and a beard."

How to Make a Child Chuckle

As the ultimate funhog uncle, your prime mission in life is to make your nephews and nieces show their teeth. In case you're ever at a loss for something funny to do, consult the following chart for evoking broad smiles and noisy laughter in little ones.

Age	Things to Do	Thing to Say
0–2	Make funny faces Blow raspberries on tummies	"Goo goo gaa gaa" (as if you didn't know)
3–6	Give piggyback rides Throw in the air when Mom's not looking Build sand castles	"I have a great poop joke for you!"
7–10	Play video games Have snowball fights Teach magic tricks	"I have a great fart joke for you!"
11–15	Take them to the mall, then hang back twenty yards so they can act cool and alone	"We're going to the mall!"
16 and up	Pick them up at school in your new, red BMW convertible	"How would you like this car for your birthday?"

8

THE WISE OLD UNCLE

When I turned seventeen and I got my license to drive, my great-Uncle Harry pulled me aside for a serious talk. "Russell," he said to me very seriously (which is how I knew this was to be a serious talk), "we need to have a serious talk" (just in case I had any doubt).

With that, Uncle Harry lifted his index finger into the air and asked me if I knew how many years he had been driving.

"No, Uncle Harry," I said.

"Fifty years," he said. "And you know how many times I've run out of gas, Russell?"

"No, Uncle Harry, I don't."

"Not once." (Long silence, for dramatic effect.) "And you know what my secret is, Russell?"

"No, Uncle Harry, I don't."

Bringing the index finger into play (aha!), he moved it from a forty-five-degree angle to straight up in the air, indicating, I soon learned, a half-tank of gas. "When the needle on the gas tank reads half-empty, I get a full tank of gas. Russell, if you fill up as soon the tank reads half-empty, you'll never run out of gas either."

I'm not saying I followed that advice. Or that I've ever given it a moment's thought up until now. The point is, Uncle Harry was trying to impart wisdom, and, as with gift giving, it's often the thought that counts. Still, you don't want your advice to be too stupid for today's hip nephews and nieces. So. This chapter, devoted to my dear Uncle Harry, offers a guide to avuncular-style wisdom for you to read, commit to memory, and cop as your own.

SMART SAYINGS

Pull out a few of the following pearls of wisdom whenever you feel your nieces or nephews are in need of guidance and comfort. To add power and punch to your erudition, scratch your chin, furrow your brow, and nod a lot (but not too much or the kids will think you're senile). Never drool when speaking. The Wise Old Uncle should look like a cross between Abraham Lincoln and Yoda and have a voice like James Earl Jones.

Old American Wisdom

Always try to rub up against money, for if you rub up against money long enough, some of it may rub off on you.   DAMON RUNYON

It's not whether you get knocked down. It's whether you get up again.   VINCE LOMBARDI

Love your enemies, for they tell you your faults.   BEN FRANKLIN

Even if you're on the right track, you'll get run over if you just sit there.   WILL ROGERS

No one can make you feel inferior without your consent.   ELEANOR ROOSEVELT

Astute Words from Beyond our Shores

You cannot shake hands with a closed fist.   INDIRA GANDHI

Be happy. It is a way of being wise.
COLETTE

Have patience with all things, but first of all with
yourself. ST. FRANCIS OF SALES

Confucius Says

Forget James Earl Jones. These are best delivered with
a Chinese accent.

It is not necessary to blow out the other person's
light to let your own shine.

What you do not want done to yourself, do not do
to others.

Contemporary Wisdom

Go back to the James Earl Jones voice.

Argue for your limitations, and sure enough,
they're yours. RICHARD BACH

Money is better than poverty, if only for financial
reasons. WOODY ALLEN

The first duty of a revolutionary is to get away with it.
ABBIE HOFFMAN

It ain't over till it's over.
                                        YOGI BERRA

Borderline Wisdom

What, me worry?   ALFRED E. NEUMAN

If we don't succeed, we run the risk of failure.
                                        DAN QUAYLE

From Sources Unknown

It is better to light a candle than to curse the darkness.

Love your enemy—it'll drive him nuts.

Rich or poor, it's good to have money.

*You can pick your friends, and you can pick your
nose, but never pick your friends' noses.*

SMART DOINGS

My father's best buddy when I was growing up was a man
named Fred Bohm, who died about fifteen years ago. He
was like an uncle to me. During my childhood, Fred
owned and operated a print shop; he was also the Robin
Hood of suburban New York. I'll give you an example.

Back in the old days (the 1960s), an airplane ticket
from New York to anywhere else cost a fantastic sum

of money, in real dollar terms considerably more than today. Uncle Fred found it galling that the wealthy airlines would charge their customers extra for drinks. Prior to the flights in those days, you could purchase liquor tickets at the check-in counter. Fred never bought liquor tickets. He printed his own. Counterfeits. Lots of them. Not that he was a heavy drinker. He wasn't. He did it out of principle. And he would pass his little counterfeits out freely among his coach-class copassengers whenever he flew.

Some might consider that unethical, unscrupulous, perhaps even sinful, but I say, "Bravo, Uncle Fred. Bravo." Of course, my own moral framework, twisted or not, undoubtedly comes partially from Uncle Fred. If I found that I'd been given 10 cents too much change by a mom-and-pop store, I'd walk a mile to return the dime—I swear I would, as I'm sure Fred would have. But when dealing with a huge, faceless corporation, well, let's just say if I wound up in one of my dealings with an extra dime, it wouldn't exactly burn a deep hole in my conscience.

But this isn't a story about dimes, airlines, or morality, it's about uncles—and how what they do and don't do can often have a great influence upon impressionable young nephews and nieces. With this in mind, it behooves uncles to behave properly around little ones. Like, for example . . .

Blow no smoke in their eyes. Aside from the incontestable evidence that secondhand smoke hurts children's lungs, think of the role model you provide if you puff in their presence. Addiction experts say that something like 99 percent of smokers take their first drag before they turn eighteen. They do it because they want to be cool, to feel like an adult, to look like, perhaps, one of their uncles whom they admire. Maybe you.

No hanging off chandeliers. A truly alarming number of teenagers told me that their most salient uncle memory was "when Uncle So-and-so got really drunk and. . . ." Remember, your teenage niece or nephew is impressionable—and so is the windshield in his or her new car. Drunkenness in general isn't too cool. Behind the wheel, it is decidedly uncool.

Don't be a slob. Teach them to care for the Earth. Excuse the cliché, but it is their inheritance. Save the whales, fight for the rain forests, stop global warming if you have the drive. At the very least, throw your damned Snickers wrappers in the trash. And teach little ones to also.

Maintain a minimum standard of political correctness. If your elders taught you that some people are better than others because of skin color or heritage, or if they taught you that making fun of those who are physically different is fun, then those elders were just plain wrong. You be right. Prejudices aren't funny. Neither are ethnic jokes or jokes about people who must struggle through life. Instead of telling dumb

ethnic or "cripple" jokes, tell your nephews and nieces
the one about the two bigots who. . . .

COMPLEMENTING YOUR
NEPHEW'S OR NIECE'S DAD

We're not talking about complimenting Dad (as in
applauding him), but rather *complementing* Dad (as in
rounding him out).

My dad knew nothing and cared nothing about
professional sports. I'm not that much different. But
I do have vivid and deliriously happy memories of the
1969 World Series, in which all of New York was in a
state of joyful frenzy because their fresh young team,
the Mets, managed to grab the pennant. I have my
Uncle Larry and his old black-and-white television
set with the rabbit-ear antenna to thank for those
memories.

And for my children, Clay and Addie, I have this
fantasy that one summer they'll go spend a couple of
weeks with their Uncle Jon in Florida, and when they
come home—presto!—they'll know how to fix things.
Uncle Jon is the kind of guy who repairs machines by
merely staring them down. He could build a house out
of ice cream sticks, dental floss, and paper clips. If
someone hauled up the *Titanic*, Uncle Jon would tighten
a screw somewhere, turn the ignition key, and the ship
would run. Clay and Addie's dad, on the other hand,
swings a hammer and his nose bleeds.

Similarly, it would be great if my children's Uncle Patrick, a professional chef, could teach them a thing or two about the culinary arts. Not that their dad doesn't make great pancakes and a pretty mean black bean soup. He does. Beyond that, however, his kitchen talents are limited.

Anyway, you get the idea. Complement their dad. If, for example, your nephew's or niece's dad is a computer geek type, you'd be doing your little buddy a favor if you were to introduce him or her to, say, mud football, hunting for crayfish, or sailing. If their dad is a cultural wastelander, think about the value of introducing your nephew or niece to plays, concerts, and great literature.

9

THE IMAGE OF UNCLE

Of course you want to be yourself around your nephews and nieces. Who would suggest otherwise? Still, be aware that the image you portray may or may not make you someone your nephews and nieces are anxious to introduce to their friends, or take to The Holy Mall. I'm greatly indebted to the teenagers who hang out at eastern Pennsylvania's Lehigh Valley Mall for their enlightening me on the finer points of uncle cool and uncle uncool.

UNCLE ATTIRE

Very cool. White or black T-shirt underneath vest; nice khakis with white Polo shirt; sweats or parachute pants (dull colors only).

Cool. Blue jeans (medium worn, medium snug); Tommy Hilfiger stuff.

Uncool. Anything polyester; golf attire (red Izod shirt, green pants); plaids and paisleys, especially below the waist; cutoff jean shorts.

Arrrrggghhhh—stay away from me!! Black shoes and white knee socks; flip-flops; tight leather pants; Boy Scout hat; love beads.

UNCLE CAREERS

Very cool. Astronaut, FBI agent, movie producer, Navy SEAL, the president, rock star, professional athlete, manager of professional sports team, the pope, lawyer (as in criminal), doctor (like a brain surgeon).

Cool. Software game designer, Supreme Court justice, senator, fireman, cop, company CEO, lawyer (as in corporate), doctor (like in psychiatry or cardiology).

Uncool. Insurance salesman, hair stylist, librarian, guidance counselor, doctor (of proctology), telemarketer, used-car salesman, janitor at school.

Arrrrggghhhh—stay away from me!! Manager of the McDonald's where all the local kids work and eat.

UNCLE WHEELS

Very cool. Humvee, hearse, limo, BMW Z3, Corvette, sports utility vehicle, Harley Davidson motorcycle.

Cool. Jaguar, classic Mustang, Jetta (black), Jeep Wrangler, Dodge Viper, Cadillac, Lexus, VW Beetle.

Uncool. Minivan, Oldsmobile, Geo Metro.

Arrrrggghhhh—stay away from me!! A dated station wagon with fake-wood siding, an old VW "hippie bus" with peace decals and flower stickers.

UNCLE NAMES

Very cool. Rick, Brett, Rex, Jim, Jack.

Cool. Charley, Eric, Reggie, Luke, Jesse, Judd, Brian, Jed, John, Bill, Barney, Bob.

Not cool. Xavier, Edgar, Delmore, Dexter, Bertram, Sherwood, Wendell.

Arrrrggghhhh—stay away from me!! Maurice, Maynard, Norbert.

10

AN UNCLE'S COMPLETE GUIDE TO GIFT GIVING

Bringing smiles to the sweet faces of your little nieces and nephews, this is what makes whatever dough you shell out on gifts well worth it—but still, those smiles are secondary. The *real* point of gift giving is to exact revenge on your siblings for all those crimes against your person and property committed decades ago. To this end, it behooves us uncles to comparison shop for gifts that are the most fun—and obnoxious.

TOYS, TOYS, TOYS

We find eight main categories of obnoxious in this area: loud toys; toys that eat lots and lots of batteries; toys that require massive assembly; toys that have gadzillions of pieces; politically incorrect toys; nauseating toys; toys that require high-priced accessories; and sacrilegious toys.

Loud toys. Fire engines, police cars, screaming Godzillas, and a drum set (be sure it includes cymbals and a cowbell) all fit into this category.

Toys that eat lots and lots of batteries. The best options are cars, trucks, robots, or anything else that moves with the help of a remote. Not only are there lots of batteries, but the parents will go crazy trying to figure out whether it is the toy itself or the remote that has the dead batteries. Make sure the battery compartment needs to be opened with a teensy screwdriver that will disappear before each needed battery change.

Toys that require massive assembly (best if instructions come in Korean, Japanese, or Mandarin Chinese, but not English). Think of the great outdoors—swing sets, monkey bars, above-ground pools, et cetera. Some electronic gadgets and rocket sets also qualify.

Toys that have gadzillions of pieces. Puzzles, Erector sets, Legos, Mega Bloks, furnished dollhouses, and science kits are all good bets here.

Politically incorrect toys. Guns for boys. Barbie dolls for girls. The ultimate politically incorrect toy has, unfortunately, been discontinued, but perhaps you can still find one in a garage sale. It was called the Share-a-Smile Becky doll, and she was a physically challenged cousin or something of Barbie, who came with her own wheelchair and (no kidding) a wheelchair-inaccessible house!

Nauseating toys. Two categories here: Sweet-nauseating, exemplified by Teletubbies and Barney and Baby Bop videos, tapes, and accessories. Then there's repulsive-nauseating, like fart cushions, fake dog doo, rubber vomit, and plastic "ice" cubes with cockroaches inside, that sort of thing. Both categories are good options.

Toys that require high-priced accessories. A great option is a Nintendo unit, which will run your sister or brother into serious debt buying game cards for years to come. In-line skates are another good possibility: you pay about $30, but the parents are then stuck shelling out for elbow and knee pads and a helmet, which will run at least twice as much as the skates. But the best option in this category—by a long shot—are the American Girl dolls. Buy your niece a Felicity doll, for example, and the next thing you know she'll be hitting up her parents for Felicity's tea table and chairs ($98), guitar ($22), and hat and brocade slippers ($18). The AG accessories list is a virtually bottomless pit.

Sacrilegious toys. These are the perfect gifts for the children of any sisters and brothers who are whacked out on religion. Introduce a little blasphemy into their lives with a Nunzilla doll—wind it up, say three Hail Marys, and sparks fly out of the little nun's mouth. This, and other gifts guaranteed to send you on a one-way trip to Uncle Satan's house, are available through the Archie McPhee catalog. Order one by writing to P.O. Box 30852, Seattle, Washington, 98103. Or you can call 425-745-0711, or E-mail Archie at mcphee@mcphee.com. McPhee also offers a number of nauseating toys and an occasional politically incorrect item.

PETS: THE LIVING END

In the fur and fin area, by great cosmic coincidence, we also find eight categories: pets that shed; pets that smell; pets that die; pets that require 6 A.M. walks; pets that pinch and claw; pets that screech and howl; highly neurotic pets; and pets that have particularly impressive bowel movements. (Because of fear of lawsuits, we have decided to leave out pets, such as pythons and cougars, that are obnoxious because they eat neighborhood children.)*

---

* This section is meant to be humorous. *Never* buy a pet as a gift for any child unless you've talked it over with the parents and ascertained that the animal will be well cared for.

You'll note that dogs and cats make most of the lists, which undoubtedly explains their enormous popularity in America.

Pets that shed. Cats, dogs (the larger the better), certain kinds of rabbits, and long-haired rodents.

Pets that smell (or have smelly cages or litter boxes). Ponies, dogs, indoor cats, small lizards, small rodents.

Pets that die. Tropical fish, especially seahorses.

Pets that require 6 A.M. walks. Any of the more active breeds of dog, such as dalmation, greyhound, German shepherd, or Labrador retriever.

Pets that pinch and claw. Cats, dogs, iguanas, large hermit crabs, rats.

Pets that screech and howl. Dogs, cats, birds.

Highly neurotic pets. Certain birds, like parrots and toucans; many small dogs, like chihuahuas and Yorkshire terriers.

Pets that have particularly impressive bowel movements. Ponies, Saint Bernards, Great Danes, mastiffs.

11

OUR UNCLE MEMORIES

I was married high up in the World Trade Center building right off the Inner Harbor of Baltimore, on the evening of July 4, 1981. The city put on a fabulous fireworks show over the harbor, and our wedding guests had the best seats in the entire city. Kaboooom! We were watching magnificent, shattering explosions of red, white, and blue—all at eye level. It was fantastic!

My great-Uncle Harry was there. At one point during the fireworks display, he turned to my father and motioning out the window said, "Larry, you must've really shelled out a lot of dough for this." Harry had a few drinks in him, I suppose, and the alcohol mixed with a few too many cobwebs made him a bit foggy that night. What can I say? The comment is now firmly entrenched in Wild family lore.

We all, I suppose, have our uncle stories. For some of us, the stories are fun, for others, they may be mixed with melancholy. Many people I've talked to have come to the realization later in life that their uncles influenced them greatly as children, often by providing visions of adulthood quite different than those they got from parents and teachers.

Here are some uncle remembrances.

FUNHOG UNCLES

Uncle Ralph: Saturday Night Companion

As told by Keith Breininger, 37

My mother's older brother, Uncle Ralph, was always a very busy man. He ran an auction house when I was a kid and also had a farm. Despite his business, he'd have me spend two weeks with him every summer, and he'd take me with him wherever he went.

We'd usually go places on his motorcycle and, because he knew it gave me a thrill, he'd always take the most curvy back roads. Uncle Ralph was always doing things that I wanted to do. Many Saturday nights he'd take me to the car races, which I loved. As I got older, like around sixteen, he started taking me hunting. My dad wasn't a hunter.

Uncle Ralph never treated me like a pain (which I'm sure I sometimes was). No matter how busy his schedule, he'd always stop and listen when I talked and never seemed judgmental. He was always easygoing. It seemed like nothing could rile him up or stress him out.

He still has the auction house, and he's as busy as ever. I've gotten busy myself, with a family and a full-time job, but Uncle Ralph and I still see each other from time to time. I'll sometimes take my boys and stop by at one of his auctions. No matter how crazy things are, he'll always stop at some point to come over to say hello to us. And although we don't do a lot of things together, at least two weekends a year Uncle Ralph and I still head out to the woods to go hunting.

Uncle George: Laughed Till He Cried

As told by Ginny Booth, 41

Uncle George and his wife raised my mother after her mother died. Mom was nine. So even though I called Uncle George "uncle," and he really was my great-uncle, he always seemed more like a grandfather than an uncle to me.

He was such a gentleman, always polite, gracious, and thoughtful. If he met a friend of yours, for instance, he'd always remember the friend's name. And he was never moody like the rest of the world. Uncle George always seemed to be in good spirits. He was forever coming up with a joke or a funny story, and then he'd tell it and laugh so hard that his whole body would shake and tears would come to his eyes!

I remember my sister and I would go to his house, and he'd make hats out of yesterday's newspaper. For some reason, we used to call them "boomaladdie" hats. That was lots of fun.

Uncle George loved reading, especially Dickens, and he loved learning. One of his favorite pastimes was researching the roots of words. Unfortunately, he had to stop his formal education right after high school to go to work. If he had gone on to college, he would have made a wonderful schoolteacher. Instead, he worked in a dye house and later as a bookkeeper in an office. He worked there till he was ninety-two! Everyone in the office called him "Pops Gormley."

Pops Gormley/Uncle George died just last summer. He was ninety-eight. He had survived his wife and two sons. But he never got lost in sorrow. Never became self-absorbed. He was always there for other people.

Uncle Quent: Mr. Jolly (Most of the Time)

As told by Rich Laliberte, 38

My mother's brother, Quent, was always a happy guy, always laughing, always looking on the bright side of things. He was also an extrovert, the complete opposite of my dad. He loved to sing, and at family gatherings, Uncle Quent was—in fact, in his eighties, still is—the one who rallied us together to sing songs. When I was growing up, he'd often line up his own children to sing, just like the Von Trapps in *The Sound of Music*.

I grew up in Fargo, North Dakota, and Uncle Quent and his singing family were in Minneapolis, so we didn't see them all that often. One time, though, when I was eleven and my brother was ten, our parents dropped us off with them to spend an entire week. That's when I discovered that jolly Uncle Quent had a serious side, too.

My brother and I were constantly fighting, and it was certainly getting on everybody's nerves. So Uncle Quent took us aside one day and laid down the law. He told us very sternly that while we were in his house, we were not to fight. There were no threats. There didn't need to be. It was enough for us simply to see him not be jolly. I felt very embarrassed. For the remainder of that visit, my brother and I were like two little angels.

WISE OLD UNCLES

Uncle Burt: A True Sport

As told by Dan Breitberg, 46

Uncle Burt was one hell of a golf player. When I was twelve or thirteen, he started to teach me the game. "If you're gonna do it, you'll do it the way it's supposed to be done," he told me. Uncle Burt taught me not only the mechanics of hitting a ball, but he also taught me to play fair, to count every stroke, to never cheat. And he also taught me to be courteous toward other players, to be quiet when others are playing, to let people pass rather than holding them up, and to not step between the ball and cup when others are ready to putt.

I'm not quite sure if Uncle Burt intended his golf lessons to be such philosophical gems, but they were just that. To me, his lessons on fairness, courtesy, playing by the rules, and not doing things half-assed pertained not only to golf, but to life itself. They were lessons I learned and try to live by—both on the golf course and off.

Yes, I'm still playing golf today. So is Uncle Burt. He lives in Florida now, and whenever I get down there, we always go out and play. You know, after all these years, he still beats me!

Uncle George: A Sober Citizen

As told by Eli Shapiro, 23

My Uncle George, my mom's brother-in-law, is the kind of guy who doesn't ask for respect, he just gets it naturally. He's a judge in Massachusetts. I went there to spend some time with him three years ago. We went out one night to Davey's Locker, a seafood restaurant in New Bedford. Uncle George got a scotch and water. He drank it down and asked me if I wouldn't mind driving us home that night, because he was considering ordering a second. "Sure," I said.

Since this was even before our dinners came, I thought that Uncle George was being exceedingly cautious, and maybe he sensed my thoughts. "You know, Eli, those two drinks aren't going to get me drunk," he said. "But I'm a judge around here, and I can't risk getting pulled over by the police with even the slightest hint of alcohol on my breath. After all, I decide cases that involve driving while intoxicated. It just wouldn't be right for me to be anything less than a model citizen in this regard."

Ever since that day, I have never—not even once—driven after drinking. And I never will. I'm no judge, but nevertheless, I respect my Uncle George and I want to follow his lead, to be a responsible citizen myself. By the way, I only recently discovered, talking to my mom, that the night I went out with Uncle George was probably the only time in his life he ordered two drinks with dinner! Mom says that he ordered those two drinks *only* to make an impression on me. He's a smart man.

Uncle Paul: Rebel with a Cause

As told by Betsy Levin, 41

My mom's younger brother, Paul, lived in Hawaii and worked as an airline pilot for Aloha Airlines. This gave him a lot of time off, often in poor East Asian countries where he would fight for the rights of the oppressed.

Uncle Paul opened my eyes to the injustices of the world and taught me that, sometimes for the sake of justice, you need to battle the status quo. My parents were pretty apolitical. So I don't know where I would have got the strong activist/leftist leanings I have today if not for my uncle.

He disappeared in the Philippines when I was a teenager. My grandparents tried to track him down but never got any information. He never showed up again. I went on to study labor in college, became a union organizer, and then a community organizer. I wish Uncle Paul were still around. I think he'd be proud of me. I know that we'd have a lot to talk about! I'd like to let him know what a big influence he was in my life. I'm sure he never had any idea.

"CRAZY" UNCLES

Uncle Jack: Mr. Generosity

As told by Emily Green, 35

Uncle Jack was married to my father's sister. He was quite literally nuts. My dad was still a teenager when his sister married Jack, and he looked up to him as a "real man," so he was thrilled when Jack offered to drive him around in downtown Birmingham. They were in the "black" part of town, and suddenly Jack turned to Dad and said, "Let's get us some niggers!" (I really apologize for the word, but that's what he said.) Then he jumped the car onto the sidewalk and tried to run down a bunch of poor pedestrians. Thank God no one was hurt, but I think my dad may have wet his pants.

Much of what I know about Uncle Jack is colored by the perceptions of a young girl who was sheltered from the seedier aspects of reality. Jack came to our house quite a bit when I was young, always bearing expensive gifts. Once he gave me a whole set of folders for collecting pennies, and most of the slots were filled already, some with rather old and rare coins. He told me to hide them and not tell anyone I had them. Another time he took my brother and me shopping for Christmas and bought us whatever we wanted—tricycles, toys, et cetera. My mom was horrified and said we could never go shopping with him again. It was only as an adult that I found out why—Jack was using other people's credit cards. I guess the penny collection must have been stolen as well.

Jack was a rough-and-ready–looking guy with a tattoo on his forearm of a scantily clad girl. He could ripple his muscles and make her dance, much to the delight of all the little kids in the neighborhood. I remember a camping trip when I was quite young, sitting around a fire while Jack taught me how to read the cards in his marked deck. Then later I watched him play poker with a bunch of strangers and win a stack of money. Being with Uncle Jack made me feel terribly grown-up and adventuresome.

On the other hand, I was actually quite terrified of Jack at times. He drank a lot, and he was a mean, loud drunk. He was eventually banned from our house for terrorizing us kids and bellowing curse words at us.

Jack met an appropriate fate. He and some buddies tried to rob a liquor store, and the shopkeeper shot at them. Jack was wounded, and apparently his "friends" just took off and left him. By the time he was found, he had bled to death. I don't really know anything else about Jack, his upbringing, or anything about what made him into what he was. Almost everyone who knew him is now dead, and those who are still around don't want to talk about him. I guess I'll never know the whole story of Uncle Jack.

Uncle Max: A Real Pistol

As told by Jim Hall, 77

Most of my uncles were pretty pale characters, but great-Uncle Max was a pistol. In his late teens, he ran away from home and fought with Pershing in Mexico. I never met him, but his exploits are part of family history.

In Max's days, gentlemen wore sidearms, especially in the South. When Uncle Max returned home from

Mexico, complete with sidearm, he went one night to a theater where some late nineteenth-century melodrama was playing. Uncle Max sat in a box and watched the villain persecute the heroine until, as any gentleman would be, he was moved to come to her rescue. He hauled out the trusty Colt and got off three shots at the villain before some cad wrested the pistol out of his hand. The men in my family have always been marksmen. Uncle Max disgraced us by missing with all three shots. The family believes that perhaps he had imbibed a dram or two before going to the theater that evening.

My father, who had known Uncle Max, told me the story. I was about twelve at the time. Dad had a quirky sense of humor, but when he was having you on there was a certain look in his eyes which I learned to detect early. I did not see that look when he told me about Uncle Max, so I really do believe the story happened. In any case, Uncle Max was the first drama critic in the Hall family. Also the last.

NEAR AND DEAR UNCLES

Uncle Mac: Exuding Charm

As told by Toni Goldfarb, 53

He was born in 1900, he never married, but rather lived with his mother, my grandmother, for most of his life.

He had many short-lived relationships with women, moving from floozie to floozie, and otherwise contenting himself with a quart of whiskey and three packs of unfiltered Camels a day. He finally died of emphysema ("ethel-seem-a," he called it), but not till he was eighty-nine. As someone at his funeral said of old Uncle Mac, "I think all that whiskey and all those cigarettes kept him pickled. As soon as he gave them up, his body fell apart—and boom, he died."

Toward the end, I was his caregiver. Looking after Uncle Mac fell upon me as the sole surviving female in my father's entire family. At first I did so out of pure obligation and pity, but darn it if that funny guy didn't get to me after a while. Toward the end, I started to feel a real fondness for Uncle Mac.

I still can't figure that out—he was amazingly cheap, not very honest, physically unappealing (poor hygiene), often unpleasant to be around (that constant smoking and drinking!), and all in all was a rather sad case. But as his floozies must have found, he did have some charm. He grew on you.

Uncle Mike: My Personal Sanity Guard

As told by Fran Gaal, 50

When I was being raised in a strict Catholic environment, being fed all kinds of bullshit by teachers and nuns, it was Uncle Mike, my mother's younger brother, who got me through it. He was the only adult who ever made any sense to me. And as my wife recently pointed out, probably no other person in my life has influenced me as much as Uncle Mike.

He always told things the way they were. He'd state his opinions on even the most taboo subjects, like religion. This drove many around him, such as my grandfather, absolutely nuts. I remember the two of them having vicious fights on the front porch, yelling and screaming at each other at the top of their lungs.

Uncle Mike was eventually thrown out of the church and so, years later, was I. I've become a lot like him in other ways too. I'm often perfectly blunt with people, sharing obvious truths, even on sensitive subjects that most people choose not to discuss. That's probably what prompted me to become a psychotherapist and why I enjoy my job so much.

Uncle Mike, I should add, was always pretty blunt with me. It was he, for instance, who first told me about sex. I was twelve, headed for a Halloween party, dressed up as a girl. Uncle Mike told me we had to sit down and have a talk. And he proceeded to give me all the graphic details, about how men are driven crazy by what women have down there. "Oh, my God!" I remember saying to myself. "So, *that's* how it's done!" And thus began my libidinous days and ways.

Uncle Mike is now about seventy, and we live fairly close. He's had a near-death experience, and that's changed him. Although he still doesn't go to church, he now believes in God. But one thing about him that hasn't changed at all is his sense of humor. He has always been a very funny man. I asked him a few years ago whether he was going to make a living will, to tell the family what to do if he ever goes senile. "Fran," he responded, "I got that all covered. I have a hitman who comes to my door once a year and asks me how it's going. I say, 'Just fine, Joe.' But the day he comes and I look at him and say, 'Who the hell are you?' Joe knows exactly what to do: Pop! He'll point his gun straight ahead and shoot."

Uncle Glen: Everything an Uncle Should Be

As told by Fiona Schwartz, 54

Uncle Glen is Canadian. He went to Great Britain during the war, met Peggy, my mother's sister, and they fell in love, married, and moved to Canada. I met Uncle Glen in Scotland when I was a baby, but that was the last time I saw him until I, too, married and moved to North America when I was twenty. A few months after arriving in the United States, my husband took me to Canada to see my Aunt Peggy and Uncle Glen.

And what a wonderful uncle he turned out to be!

Growing up I had other uncles in my life, but none who hold a special place in my heart like Uncle Glen does. From that first visit, he welcomed us as he would his own children. He took my husband on his first hunting trip. Quite an adventure for a boy from Brooklyn.

Uncle Glen grew up on a farm in rural Ontario, one of seven boys and three girls. They learned at an early age to work hard, but always found time for fun too. He always, for instance, has a good joke to tell—most of them a little bawdy.

We would visit Canada almost every summer and when our children came along, Uncle Glen was there to buy them their first fishing rods. He would take them fishing for sunfish. Some days he would chase the kids around the yard, and when he caught them, he'd give them whisker rubs, making them scream with delight. He taught us all to play cribbage, and he'd try to cheat us on the score—just in fun, of course.

Some thirty years later, we still love to visit Uncle Glen. He is everything an uncle should be and then some!

HERO UNCLES

Uncle Charlie: Ace Bombardier

As told by Lewis Schmidt, 67

He was my mother's half-brother, only ten years older than me. From the time I was an infant until I was eleven or twelve, Uncle Charlie and I shared a room. In fact, we shared a bed. He was more like an older brother than anything else. Uncle Charlie was always a good student, well behaved and well liked.

When World War II started, he went overseas as a tail-gunner, later became a bombardier, and wound up flying seventy-six missions. I was very proud of him. I remember once buying him a record he'd asked me for—"Boogie Woogie" by Tommy Dorsey, I think—to send to him in Europe. I accidentally sat on the record, and it broke! I'm sure I replaced it and eventually mailed it off.

Both before and after the war, Uncle Charlie and I would get up at two in the morning on the first day of trout season to run down to the river. We did that every year until I was in my forties.

Charlie is now seventy-seven, and he doesn't live far from me. We still have a good relationship, but we don't see each other a lot. He's grown very reserved and quiet over the years. I think that's probably due to his war experience, flying all those missions, never knowing when his life would end. He also lost a child some years ago, and there is nothing in life as rough as that.

I don't think I ever consciously strived to be like Uncle Charlie, but I'm sure on some level he rubbed off on me and had something to do with making me the person I am.

Uncle Davey: The Bronx Bull

As told by Larry Wild (the author's father), 72

Uncle Davey was my mother's brother and—how shall I say this?—not too smart a man. But he was the toughest guy I ever knew, small, but strong as an ox. He was a pro boxer for a few years. Then he got a job as a fitness instructor with the FBI somewhere down in the Carolinas.

One day before he got that job, I was sitting on the curb on the Grand Concourse in the Bronx, tying my shoes, which were brand new. I was probably nine years old. It was fall, because I remember all the leaves were off the trees. Along came this gang of teenagers, and they started taunting me. One of them grabbed one of my shoes, pulled down a young tree, tied the shoe to the top, and let the tree spring up so that the shoe was out of my reach. Then he and his buddies laughed at me while I jumped up and down trying to snatch the shoe.

That's when I heard a familiar voice and turned around to see my Uncle Davey. "Lawrence," he said, "what's going on here?" And I started to cry. The next thing I knew, Davey grabbed one of the teenagers in a headlock. Most of the teenagers ran, but one of them got brave and turned back to help his friend. Davey swung his arm over the kid's head and got him in a headlock too. And with one boy under each arm, he then started knocking their heads together, like two coconuts.

It seemed like a good time before Davey let the boys go, and they weren't in such hot condition by that time. They stumbled off like two drunks. A little later, the police came rapping on our door, asking for Davey. My father was good friends with a local councilman and ran to see him to have him pull some strings for Uncle Davey. I don't know what would have happened to my uncle if my dad hadn't had that political connection.

As for the teenagers, I saw them again and they saw me again, many times. But they never again would dare to come within twenty yards of me!

Uncle John: A True Giant

As told by Joan Mastel, 64

My favorite uncle was six-foot-four-inches tall. Growing up we were all told to eat, so we could grow big like Uncle John, my mother's brother. He would put a hand on each side of our heads and lift us up high in the air, very frightening but something we all thought was very special, 'cause it was Uncle John doing it. My little cousins would tell all their friends, "Our Uncle John is so big and so strong he could lift this whole house and set it out in the street." And all the little eyes would grow huge just thinking about being able to meet him. To all of us little people, he was a giant. He passed away last fall and, although he was ill and couldn't get around too good, he was still a giant among men. One of the last things he gave me was a $2 bill. I carry that bill with me wherever I go, and I wouldn't spend it or part with it for anything.

OTHERWISE INFLUENTIAL UNCLES

Uncle Don: A Special Guy in More Ways Than One

As told by Debra Kaplan, 39

I suppose I was something like four or five when I began to realize that Uncle Don was different from other adults. My father's younger brother, I discovered, was mentally retarded. He lived with my grandparents, and we'd see him once a week and vacation with him in the summers. He'd tease me and my sister a lot, calling us "Pest #1," and "Pest #2." Probably because he was mentally challenged, he could in some ways relate to kids better than other adults could. I remember him as lots of fun to be around.

There was also something intriguing about Uncle Don, because he was different. More than anything else, I believe, it was my interest in Uncle Don and his uniqueness that led me to choose a career as a special education teacher.

Uncle Dana: No Shining Light

As told by "Noah," 38

I have a story, not very pleasant, and I wouldn't want my name attached, but it taught me a lot.

My Uncle Dana (husband of my father's sister) grew up extremely poor, one of twelve kids in a rural family in Maine. He was and is an incredible character—absolutely adored by women, was an amazing water skier and a hell of a drinker. They had two kids, a boy and a girl. Dana worked installing traffic lights. Then, he and another guy got the bright idea to start their own company. The other guy couldn't take the pressure, but Dana hung in there, and soon this company that installed traffic lights was the biggest in the Northeast. Dana was wealthy—not a multimillionaire, but surely his take was in the quarter-mill ballpark every year.

Still, Dana was Dana, and the drinking and the womanizing kept up. My aunt stuck by him through it all, but Dana has just continued into a downward spiral. He's now a barely functioning alcoholic with almost no contact with his family. Somehow he keeps the business together, but even that is dicey. Meanwhile, his son already has several DUIs and is being sued for a fraternity drinking party that resulted in another kid's death. His daughter is heading down the same road. Dana's collection of antique cars, his cabin on the lake—all of it is in ruins.

That taught me an important lesson. It taught me that life is a long journey, and that you have to aim for success on a lot of different levels over a long period of time. I always thought Dana was cooler than my father, and I wanted to be like him—high living and rich. Now I see my dad—mid-fifties, retired, healthy, looks like he's forty, still very much in love with my mom—and I see which one of them is really successful. Whenever I'm tempted to do something stupid, I think of those two and I know which course I should take.

Uncle Charles: Brilliance Gone Asunder

As told by Gwendolyn Allen, 56

When I was going through school, teachers of mine would talk about how brilliant my dad and my Uncle Charles were. Uncle Charles played classical piano and violin. My dad, who was just a couple of years older, was a mathematician and a poet. They were the Baptist minister's sons, and everyone in town expected a whole lot of them.

Maybe, in part, it was because of those heavy expectations that my father and my uncle both wound up alcoholics. Both of their families disintegrated as a result. And both brothers died early of alcohol-related diseases. Uncle Charles was sixty-one. I flew out to Chicago for the funeral. I've always felt sad about him, so much potential and none of it realized.

I had a glass of champagne for New Year's. That's the only drink I've had all year. My two kids are the same way. I've told them over the years, "You *don't* drink." I'm convinced that in some families, like ours, there's a genetic predisposition to alcoholism. If it had just been my dad with the problem, I might not have become aware of that. But the fact that both he and my Uncle Charles had the same problem makes me positive that genetics is involved.

SINGLE-THEME UNCLES

All My Uncles: Zzzzzzz

As told by Marc Nissenbaum, 50

I remember all my uncles the same way—as a bunch of guys who'd sleep on the couch while the cousins played.

Uncle Martin: The Dentist's Best Friend

As told by Bob Gordon, 51

When Uncle Martin would come to see us—in fact, *every* time he came to see us—he would bring me lots of Chiclets.

Uncle Sid: Predictable Guy

As told by Shirley Morganelli, 49

I had an Uncle Sid who was married to my Aunt Boop (my mother's sister). Every time he saw me he would look at me and say, "Ickle pickle." That is literally the only thing he ever said to me, but he said it every time. I never thought it was strange though, and I really liked him.

CONCLUSION:
GIVING UNCLES THEIR DUE

Sara Ann Cunningham ends her book, *Aunts*, with a lament that aunts in our society don't get enough respect. She aptly points out that we have a Mother's Day and a Father's Day, and January 22 is National School Nurse Day. So what about an Aunt's Day, huh? Isn't it high time?

I could live with an Aunt's Day. Women are easy to shop for. But I shudder to think of a National Uncle's Day. It would inevitably result in the buying of millions of sweaters and loud ties, which would sit in men's closets along with gadzillions of other sweaters and loud ties, resulting only in increased profits for L. L. Bean and Hallmark, and a bunch of moths in need of Weight Watchers.

But I do think, absolutely, that uncles don't get enough respect in our society. Forget about there being no Uncle's Day. Just look in any bookstore. Why have there been so many books (scholarly and popular, fiction and nonfiction) on the Civil War—and only this one on uncles? Why are movies and documentaries on the Civil War also so popular, and yet there are so few on uncles? Did the Civil War ever bounce you on its knee? Or buy you ice cream? Or give you a piggyback ride? Is the Civil War anyone you could talk to about your rotten parents? Or someone you can go to the park with and chuck a football? Do you have pictures of the Civil War in your family album?

Of course not. So, what gives?

I don't know. But I suggest we can begin to correct the injustice by telling our uncles right now how much we appreciate them and how much more important they are to us than the Civil War. Just don't do it with a sweater and loud tie, okay?

BIBLIOGRAPHY

My good professors in college taught me that every serious book must wrap up with a bibliography—a listing of literature that the author used in his research, as well as a suggestion of readings for those who wish to learn more about the subject at hand. Since there is no—absolutely no—body of literature on uncles (which I find frustrating as a researcher and insulting as an uncle), and since this book is not all that entirely serious, I've decided to make up my own bibliography. Just make it up. Every bit of it.

So, here is my fantasy bibliography—a collection of scholarly and popular articles, books, and dissertations about uncles, the kind that would exist in a just world, a fair world, a world where uncles were fully recognized for their many and varied contributions to civilization.

Dunn, H. "Consequences of uncles throwing young children up in the air, including the effects on parental sanity and the adult sibling relationship." *Annual Review of Avuncular Research* 1997, 25(2): 184–198.

Freud, S. "The role of piggyback rides in the formation of the Id" (1922). In *The Collected Lectures on Psychosocial Exploration*. London: Hogarth, 1950.

Geraci, B. "Men who watch football and make grunting sounds: A Darwinian approach to the understanding of the uncle." *Journal of Abnormal Relative Psychology* 1998, 20:23–35.

Hufe, M. "The uncle as a primary source of sugary treats leading to dental decay in pediatric and adolescent populations." *Journal of the American Dental Association* 1996, 23(5):1487–1499.

Kasparov, G. *An Invitation to the "Got Your Nose" Game for Uncles: Rules and Strategies*. New York: Fireside, 1999.

Kuffleberg, A. "The role of noogies in early childhood development." *Annual Review of Avuncular Research* 2000, 37(5):193–201.

Littman, J., and Littman, M. "Was Uncle Martin really from Mars, or was he a delusional psychotic with fake antennae?" *Journal of the American Psychological Association* 1997, 26(9):293–299.

Loewen, J. *Lies Your Uncle Told You About His Role in WWII: For Example, Eisenhower Did Not Shine Your Uncle's Shoes.* New York: McGraw-Hill, 1996.

Marx, K. *Die Onkels und Stupidfartenjokens.* London: Das Kapital Press, 1868.

McDonald, C., and McDonald, L. *Uncles and Their Oldsmobiles: A Pictorial History.* Vol. 861 of *Men and Their Automobiles.* Washington, D.C.: Time-Life Publications, 1993.

Montegue, A. *Uncle Fester: The Legend and the Man.* Vol. 945 of *Great American Biographies.* Washington, D.C.: Time-Life Publications, 1992.

Morganelli, S. *And They Continued to Play Poker: Uncles on the* Titanic. New York: Little Brown, 1992.

Nietzsche, F. *Thus Spake Zarathustra's Uncle Hans* (1884). In *The More Than Complete Anthologies of Freidrich Nietzsche and Sons.* Oxford: Oxford University Press, 1969.

O'Brien, P. "Uncles whirling children by the ankles and the risk of cranial fracture." *The American Journal of Orthopaedic Malpractice and Golf.* July 1996, 321:450–455.

Perrine, S. "Where can you meet a man like Uncle Fester?" *Cosmopolitan*, June 1999.

Pirsig, R. *The Role of the Uncle in Vehicular Maintenance*. New York: John Wiley, 1998.

Potts, T. *Giggling Children: What Happens When Uncles Pass Gas*. Cambridge, MA: Harvard University Press, 1997.

Sartre, J. *Being, Nothingness, and My Uncle Pierre: An Essay in Phenomenological Uncology* (1944; Eng. trans. 1957; preface by Maurice Chevalier). New Haven, CT: Yale University Press, 1957.

Starr, K. *Overly Indulgent Uncles as a Root of Child Misbehavior and Adult Depravity*. Washington, D.C.: Georgetown University Press, 1999.

Tocqueville, A. *Uncles in America*. (2 vols., 1841, 1843; Eng. trans. 2 vols., 1842–1844; preface by Jackie Coogan). Paris: Livres d'Oeuf, 1842–1844.

Vaughn, R., Candy, J., Coogan, J., and the editors of *Uncles* magazine. *The Complete Guide to Uncling: Thousands of Tips Any Guy Can Use to Spoil a Nephew or Niece*. Emouse, PA: Rodeo Press, 1997.

Wild, R. "Uncles and their propensity to wear plaid: A psychological analysis." *Annual Review of Avuncular Research* 2000, 33(6):248–267.

Wild, R. *They Had Season Passes to the Colosseum: Uncles of Ancient Rome.* Cambridge: Cambridge University Press, 1997.

Wild, R. *They Cheered the Crusades and Booed the Infidels: Uncles of the Medieval Era (1350–1500).* Cambridge: Cambridge University Press, 1995.

ABOUT THE AUTHOR

Among Russell Wild's other roles in life—husband, father, contributor to numerous national magazines, mean in-line skater, and boomerang thrower—he is proud also to be an uncle. Uncle Russ, a native New Yorker, now lives in Allentown, Pennsylvania. His one niece and various and sundry nephews are divided between the two coasts. Other books by the author include *Why Men Marry*, *Games Bosses Play*, and *Career Smarts*. He has appeared many times on radio and television, including spots on *Oprah*, *The View*, *CBS Morning News*, and *Good Day New York*. He can be reached at Rwild@Compuserve.com.